FENG SHUI

FENG SHUI

ARRANGING YOUR HOME TO CHANGE YOUR LIFE

KIRSTEN M. LAGATREE

FOREWORD BY ANGI MA WONG

Illustrations by Frank Paine

Villard / New York

Villard Books is a registered trademark of Random House, Inc.

Library of Congress Cataloging-in-Publication data is available.
ISBN 679-76543-3

Manufactured in the United States of America on acid-free paper
9

Book design by JoAnne Metsch

*This book is dedicated
to my husband,
John Barth,
who attracts good chi wherever he goes*

FOREWORD

WELCOME TO THE FASCINATING WORLD OF FENG SHUI, THE ANCIENT
Chinese art of placement.

The maintenance of harmony and balance in the universe and
in nature is the fundamental goal of feng shui. This may seem like a
tall order, but it is absolutely in our control; humans' relationship
with the environment and our respect for nature are at the very crux
of feng shui. All living things—people, the earth, the universe—are
interrelated by cosmic energy (chi). Very simply put, nothing hap-
pens without consequence to something else. This has been the Asian
way throughout the centuries, in contrast to the "I came, I saw, I con-
quered" philosophy of Western civilization.

In the realm of feng shui, the woes of mankind and the world
can be seen as the direct result of humans' disrespect for the laws of
the universe and our failure to take care of the planet. Today more
than ever, with our ozone depleted, rain forests disappearing, oceans

and air polluted, and land overdeveloped, it is no wonder that Mother Earth retaliates with a plethora of natural disasters.

Feng shui has its roots in ancient China, where it was believed that the spirits of ancestors were able to help their living descendants, and so it was crucial for Chinese families to honor their deceased by finding the best possible burial locations for them. Temples, homes, and businesses were also carefully sited to harmonize with the energies of the land, in order to attract good luck, health, and fortune. The streets of towns and cities were laid out according to these principles of placement as the Chinese established communities all over the world.

While the practice of feng shui has been common in Chinese communities for centuries, it is rapidly gaining popularity in many Western countries. Many non-Asians are turning to feng shui in an effort to return to what feels natural and right—perhaps in reaction to the conspicuous consumption of what I call the Excessive Eighties, and to the intrusion of technology in their lives. The continuing and growing concern with environmental issues, the health and exercise boom, the surge in alternative medicine, and the explosive growth in home gardening are all indicative of the same trend. Feng shui can be, to borrow Club Med's slogan, an "antidote to civilization," providing peace and serenity in a complex age of change, confusion, and stress.

Practicing feng shui is a return to intuitive living: What feels right is right, what needs attention receives it. By adjusting our balance with the world around us, we are able to direct our lives toward our goals and aspirations. In an era in which technology and a fast-paced life threaten to control us, we can resume control of our lives through understanding our environment rather than "conquering" it.

Consider a few examples:

In the saltwater aquarium in my office, a water pump had been inoperative for many months. Finally, on a free morning, I cleaned it of crystallized salt, replaced the magnet inside the motor, and—with

a whoosh—restarted it with a strong, bubbly flow of water in the tank.
I was away from my office for the remainder of the day, and when I
returned there were *ten* messages on my voice mail, many of which
resulted in media interviews and contracts for my intercultural con-
sulting business. The rapidly circulating water, representing wealth
and business success, had activated those aspects of my life. By paying
attention to the problems of my aquarium—a mini-environment of its
own—I had jump-started my business life as well as the water pump.

One Portland woman was plagued by neighbors with screaming
children and a barking dog. She purchased a lucky eight-sided mirror
at one of my seminars and installed it on the outside wall of her
house, facing her noisy neighbors. Within a day, the ruckus ceased,
but even more astonishing was her report to me several months later:
The undesirable neighbor, who had sworn that he would never move
from Portland, the city where he had lived and worked for eighteen
years, declared that he and his family were selling their home and
moving away. The mirror had deflected the negative energy originat-
ing from them *back to them.*

Another elderly workshop attendee claimed that the house she
had inherited was trying to kill her, as she had suffered several accidents since moving there. I suggested she have her house painted in
colors corresponding to the principles of feng shui, bringing the
building into harmony with its location. When I returned to her city
five months later, she came to see me with a story of feng shui in
action: "My neighbors got together to paint my house free of charge,
and now, every time I go home, I feel as if twenty-seven sets of arms
are hugging me," she said. Not only was her house better adjusted to
its site, but her sense of being at home there was aided by the gen-
erosity of her neighbors.

One client told me that her business had suddenly come to a
halt four months earlier, and that she wanted to revive it. Moreover,
she was eager to revive her social life and start dating. I spent several
hours assessing her home and noticed a worn armchair in her living

room, where it blocked the front door. It was from the set of a movie about a serial killer, and she had brought it into her house four months before. I explained that the furniture had negative energy, symbolizing death, and it was affecting her business and her love life. The armchair had to go. Together we moved the armchair from the living room, struggling to lift it and manipulate it through the front door and onto the patio. The very minute that the chair went through the door, the woman's telephone rang. It was an acquaintance calling to make a date.

Later she called me with a progress report: "The chair's been gone for weeks, and my entire home feels so vibrant and different every time I step into the living room. My business has picked up, and socially I'm busier than I've ever been." In moving the chair, my client had not only removed negative energy, but she had opened up a blocked front door, allowing for an increased energy flow, and opened her life to many successes.

Feng shui was always a part of my Chinese upbringing (I grew up in Taiwan and New Zealand and spent summers in Hong Kong). Curiosity and a lifelong love of knowledge directed me to seek out more on the subject, and I found that there are as many variations of the practice as there are books, teachers, classes, and believers. What Kirsten Lagatree presents here, and what I have developed as a result of my own experience, background, research, and intuition, is a method of *practical* feng shui, which combines elements of several schools. The approach is an eclectic one, drawing from many sources yet not favoring any one in particular—there are those who study feng shui under a "master" or in a "school" who most likely will consider this both unorthodox and blasphemous. However, I have found this practical method of feng shui successful for myself and my clients, and I can attest to its effectiveness in bringing many positive things to my life and to the lives of others. The use of traditional feng shui tools—colors, numbers, animal symbols, and elements—in arranging furniture and accessories helps harmonize both home and work environments, and rearranging rooms using feng shui principles enables the energy flow to move differently, facilitating change.

As Ralph Waldo Emerson said, "There is no knowledge that is not power." Learning feng shui will empower you to effect positive changes in your life. In this book, Kirsten Lagatree offers an infinitely readable, uncomplicated, and above all *practical* primer for learning and using the ancient art of feng shui. You'll be amazed at the doors it will open for you.

—ANGI MA WONG

ACKNOWLEDGMENTS

I OWE A DEBT OF GRATITUDE TO MANY WHO HAVE BEEN BOTH PATIENT
and generous in initiating me to the ways of feng shui. Special thanks
to Dick Barnes, my editor at the *Los Angeles Times,* who first sent me
on this journey, and to Laura Lee, my first guide. Thanks also to Crystal Chiu and Dalana Leong of the Yun Lin Temple, Louis Audet,
Ashley Dunn, Johndennis Govert, Kartar Khalsa, Peter and Jenny
Lee, James Moser, Kathryn Metz, Steven Post, and, of course, my
friend and teacher Angi Ma Wong.

Thanks also to those who have shared their personal experiences
and adventures in the practice of feng shui: Edward Carson Beale,
Casey Caves, Kristin Frederickson, Bruce Goff, Jeanne Gucciardi,
Annie Kelly, Sam Lee, Helen Luk of the American Feng Shui Institute, Marina McDougall, Carol Meltzer, Joan Malter Osburn, Joy
Ou, Eva Sax, Sharon Tedesco, Janet Tunick, Helga Weiss, and Steve
Wilson. Thanks to Karen Lesico and Jean Houts of the Eugene

O'Neill Tao House, and to Leslie Ehrman of the American Society of Interior Designers for their help and expertise.

I feel deep appreciation and affection for several friends who have gone out of their way to provide me with support and assistance: Andy Black, Adele Borman, Jennifer Cockburn, Connie Goldman, Shobana Kokatay, George Lewinski, Harry Lin, David Pendlebury, Louis G. Perez, Lee and Barbara Shoag, David Stone, Harriet Williams, and Henry Wong. Thanks to my friend Catherine Carlisle, for her support and detailed comments on parts of the manuscript. And much gratitude goes to writer and friend Jan Burke, who rallied my spirits and helped me solve many mysteries of publishing along the way.

Thanks to Frank Paine, illustrator and visionary, whose skill as an artist is exceeded only by his wacky sense of humor and talent for friendship. My agent, Nancy Yost, deserves recognition for being smart, tough, and funny—always at just the right moment. Many thanks go to my meticulous, creative, and supportive Villard editor, Page Dickinson. Thanks also to Villard publicity manager Suzanne Wickham-Beaird for her enthusiasm.

Special thanks to my husband, John Barth, who calmly took over many household duties when frenzy overtook me. Heartfelt thanks to the Literary Women of Long Beach, who have surrounded me with love, encouragement, and support for many years. Love and gratitude to Bruce, Marion, and Donald Lagatree, who cheered me on. And most particular appreciation and affection go to my wonderful parents-in-law, John and Pat Barth, for being proud of me.

CONTENTS

INTRODUCTION

HAVE YOU EVER WALKED INTO SOMEONE'S HOUSE AND FELT INSTANTLY at home? Was it the furniture that created a welcoming atmosphere? The shape of the room? The way the light came in the windows? Perhaps you couldn't quite put your finger on it, but everything just felt right. Maybe you felt "good vibes," warm hospitality, or a perfect balance between comfort and style.

Quite possibly what you experienced was good feng shui (pronounced "fung shway"). A home with good feng shui radiates serenity. The building, its furnishings, and consequently its inhabitants are in harmony with nature.

The location of a building, the arrangement of its furniture and contents, and the use of color within each room—all these factors contribute to an environment that is balanced or unbalanced, energizing or enervating, positive or negative. By following the rules of feng shui, the ancient Chinese art of placement, you can work with these basic elements—color, furniture, artwork, plants, room shape, and location—to create a balanced environment in any building, home, or office.

The literal meaning of *feng shui* is "wind and water"—a kind of shorthand for "natural surroundings." Years ago, the Chinese were ruled by nature in their everyday lives; as you learn the principles of feng shui described in this book, you'll see that much of this ancient Chinese craft is drawn from basic rules for thriving in sometimes hostile environments. For modern practitioners, feng shui provides a means of controlling and balancing one's surroundings in a way that brings happiness, prosperity, and health.

There are many schools of feng shui and, within each, many methods of practicing this ancient art for modern times. The oldest school, known as the Land Form (or simply Form) School, dates back to the Tang dynasty (A.D. 618–907). From its origin in the jagged mountains of southern China, the Form School uses hills, mountains, rivers, and other natural land formations as a basis to evaluate the quality of a location. (However, the earliest recorded reference to feng shui comes from the Han dynasty [202 B.C.–A.D. 220]. *The Canon of Dwellings*, written in this period, was used to site tombs and the palaces of emperors.)

As feng shui gained in popularity it spread well beyond southern China, first to the north and eventually to other regions and countries. Gradually, the practice of feng shui evolved to accommodate these new, often urban, environs. Today feng shui masters rarely rely solely on land masses to analyze a location. In fact, the adaptability of this ancient craft is demonstrated by the fact that its modern practice includes tips on the placement of televisions, computers, and other electronic equipment. But many of the Form School's ideas were absorbed into theories that came later, and the Form School's observations about the way pure geography influences quality of life remain at the core of feng shui as it is practiced today.

About a century after the Form School was developed, some students of feng shui began using a compass, along with complex astronomical and astrological calculations, to evaluate the feng shui of a site. The Compass, or Fukien, School evolved in the flat plains of northern China in direct response to the problem of analyzing an area that had few major topographical features. This school introduced the idea that specific points of the compass exert unique influences on various aspects of life. For example, the south, with its orientation toward the sun's path and away from cold north winds, was declared a most auspicious direction, particularly conducive for achieving longevity, fame, and fortune. Rooted in the same natural world as the Form School, but allowing for easier use of feng shui in a variety of locations, the Compass School represented a step in the evolution of the feng shui that we practice today.

Finally, a third major, and much more recent, school of feng shui was developed in the last fifty years by the feng shui master Lin Yun in Berkeley, California. As the feng shui movement grew in the United States, Professor Lin saw a need to make the ancient practice accessible to more people and adaptable to more situations. Consequently, he created the Black Hat Sect Tantric Tibetan Buddhist method of feng shui. The Black Hat Sect uses the front door of a building or the main door of a room as a starting point for analyzing a location's feng shui. Where the older school requires a compass to determine which parts of a room represent important life issues, Professor Lin's method locates these critical areas in relation to the doorway. Because of its simplicity and accessibility, the Black Hat Sect has become very popular in the West.

This book draws on the best of each school to present a practical, easy-to-follow guide to the art of feng shui. You will gain a good basic knowledge of the principles of feng shui and learn how to put them to work in your home or office. You'll also learn about common interior-design mistakes that can cause bad feng shui, negatively affecting your attitude, your energy level, and even the most intimate details of your personal and professional life. Most important, you'll learn cures that can neutralize negative influences and help you achieve health, prosperity, and peace of mind.

Using this practical guide you can analyze and transform your home room by room. From the master bedroom to the kitchen to the study, you will learn techniques for creating harmony and balance in your surroundings. Feng shui isn't magic, but when you use it properly, you will feel its effects in your life.

FENG SHUI

FENG SHUI: WHAT IT IS, WHERE IT COMES FROM, HOW IT WORKS

FENG SHUI OFFERS A CHANCE TO GAIN A LITTLE ADVANTAGE IN THAT celestial chess game known as destiny. Geomancy, as feng shui is also called, is the art of manipulating one's physical surroundings for the purpose of nudging fate in a favorable direction.

The goal of feng shui is nothing less than to achieve balance between the forces of yin and yang, the two opposite but complementary forces of the universe, through the proper arrangement of the objects within and around your home. In this book you will learn to mix and match the five elements—earth, water, fire, metal, and wood—along with colors and shapes to create balance and harmony in your personal environment.

Think of feng shui as a cross between art and science, with its roots in ecology, aesthetics, philosophy, astrology, and interior design. It transcends the confines of rational thought and the rigid realm of logic, yet is firmly grounded in common sense and scientific observation. The San Francisco interior designer Joan Malter Osburn puts it this way: "It's about feeling comfortable in a space, psychologically as well as physically. A room that looks good and is functional is going to have good feng shui."

SOME HISTORY

AT LEAST THREE THOUSAND YEARS AGO, FARMERS IN SOUTHERN CHINA developed certain feng shui principles because of their dependence on the earth and the forces governing it. They found that living in harmony with nature made life much easier, and they learned the hard way that upsetting the balance of their environment brought on disasters.

Homes built in river valleys were regularly lost to floods, while villages nestled among the hills were not only protected from the elements, but were easier to defend from attackers than low-lying towns. Hence, hillside homes were considered most desirable. The ancient Chinese found that buildings facing north bore the brunt of noxious storms of yellow dust that blew down from Mongolia. Also, north-facing dwellings were less hospitable because they weren't situated to maximize the warmth of the sun. Consequently, south-facing buildings came to be regarded as auspicious. In fact, because feng shui was always carefully observed in siting and building imperial palaces for the emperors, the Chinese have a saying, "To face the south is to become a king."

In addition to using feng shui for the down-to-earth demands of farming and the lofty realm of housing emperors, ancient Chinese geomancers were also called in to help bury the dead. Because ancestor veneration is an important part of Chinese culture, feng shui was—and in many cases still is—extremely important for finding the best burial locations for family members. The thinking goes that well-buried forebears will be disposed to look more kindly on their relatives still struggling on earth. Ancestors made happy with the good feng shui of their tombs will shower the blessings of prosperity, honor, long life, and healthy offspring on the living.

Sylvia, a northern California accountant, became depressed and began fighting with her husband and doing poorly in her business after moving into their spacious new home. She hired a geomancer to help her diagnose the problem and discovered that their building had bad feng shui for her, in part because she had a greater need for sunlight and warmth than her north-facing home was providing.

The feng shui expert suggested specific cures that brought more light into the home, using mirrors, crystal chandeliers, and strategically placed lamps. These feng shui adjustments represented both a concrete and a symbolic approach to correcting problems; the addition of badly needed light provided both the literal and the metaphorical warmth that had been lacking since Sylvia's move to the new house.

CHI

ALTHOUGH THE CHINESE SOMETIMES REFER TO CHI AS THE COSMIC dragon's breath of the universe, *chi* can be translated more literally as energy. Chi is the invisible flow of energy that circulates through the earth and sky, bringing the life force with it. It is the essential ingredient in feng shui. Just as a building and its residents benefit from a constant flow of fresh air, nothing can flourish without a good supply of smoothly flowing chi.

The practice of feng shui is about harnessing this vital force to maximize the positive effects that it bestows. By enhancing and directing this chi flow, we are able to influence fate.

Chi travels best when it echoes nature by flowing in gentle curves, rather than shooting along straight lines or sharp edges, where it can move too quickly or be easily blocked. Man-made structures that reshape the environment—roads, tunnels, housing developments, and so forth—can adversely affect its movement, creating bad chi, or sha. Narrow openings or hallways can create unfavorable energy by causing chi to flash by so quickly that none of its beneficial effects are left behind. When it courses past angles or sharp corners, chi creates "poison arrows" that shoot harmful forces at anything in its path. Sha can bring on poor health, family quarrels, business difficulties, bad luck—any number of problems and misfortunes. If good chi is cosmic breath, think of sha as cosmically bad breath!

Just as the chi in our surroundings affects our fortunes and makes the world work the way it does, human chi animates us and makes each of us who we are. In individuals, the quality of chi governs personality as well as health and vitality. Certain Chinese practices such as meditation, martial arts exercises, and acupuncture (which uses tiny needles to redirect chi within the body) are ways of correcting and enhancing the flow of personal chi. In fact, feng shui has been referred to as "acupuncture for the home."

If you've ever had a yoga class, you've probably heard the word "prana," the life force that energizes your body as you harness and direct it with your breathing. When you arrange your home according to the principles of feng shui, you do something similar, channeling that force in a positive direction and clearing away blockages that inhibit the free flow of vitality.

Obstructed chi flow in the human body can cause problems ranging from inhibitions to illness. Its effects are very individual— whether you get sick, have problems at work, or fight with your family depends on your own unique chi. In the home, blocked chi, or sha, can disrupt the lives of the inhabitants in a wide variety of ways that include illness but extend to areas as disparate as childbirth, career and finances, marriage prospects, and relationships with friends and family.

Proper chi flow is even important while you sleep. Your bedroom should be a serene and peaceful place, but if the head of your bed is in line with the bedroom door, chances are the chi won't flow smoothly once it's inside the room. You will be surrounded by blocked and stagnant chi while sleeping, and will feel groggy and tired in the morning.

These are examples of feng shui's blend of the mystical with the logical: although the rules about bed placement at first may seem strange and mysterious, they are actually all about arranging a bedroom that will contribute to the health, happiness, and general well-being of the sleeper. And it follows that a healthy, well-rested individual who is at peace with the world will naturally be a more effective, successful, and prosperous person. So this is an example of how you can actually change your life by rearranging a room. In similar ways, you will find that observing the rules of feng shui as you approach the interior design of your home will yield a more harmonious and a more aesthetically pleasing result in every room.

A CENTRAL IDEA IN CHINESE THINKING IS THAT THE OPPOSITE FORCES of yin and yang are a fundamental fact of the universe. The relationship between yin and yang is also a key concept in feng shui. Yin is female, yang is male. Yin is dark, yang is light. Yin is passive, yang is active. Yin is the earth, the moon, receptivity, darkness, and cold. Yang is the dragon—fierce, strong, hot, moving, and living; it represents heaven and the sun. Yin is death, yang is life. These opposite forces don't line up against each other as "good" or "bad." Rather, yin and yang are complementary. They depend on each other for their very existence—without darkness there can be no light, without life there is no death. The universe requires a balance between them.

The interaction of yin and yang creates the changes that keep the world turning; summer leads to winter, night becomes day. And as we balance these forces in feng shui, we find that bad—or good— luck will turn and change according to how well balance has been achieved in our surroundings.

The principle that knits together the concepts of yin, yang, and chi is known as the Tao (pronounced "dow"), which means "the way" or "the path." Taoism is devoted to the constant seeking of harmony

YIN AND YANG

The white dot on the black portion of the yin/yang symbol and the black dot on the white section are reminders that each quality contains some of its opposite.

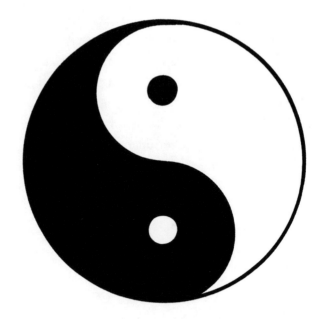

and balance, striving always to combine just the right amounts of yin and yang in all things—which is what feng shui is about.

Feng shui has its roots deep in the wisdom of the *I Ching*, known in English as *The Book of Changes*, an ancient Chinese work that is still consulted today both for practical and mystical guidance. The *I Ching*, which predates both Taoism and Confucianism and is the basis for most Chinese thought and philosophy, stresses the fundamental nature of change and flux in one's fortunes and emphasizes the link between one's destiny and the natural world. Its basic premise is that surroundings have a powerful effect on fate.

THE BA-GUA

THE FENG SHUI CHART YOU SEE ON PAGE 12 IS BASED ON THE BA-GUA, a chart that comes from the *I Ching*. This chart will be our guide as we make our way through your home in the chapters ahead. The ba-gua's octagonal shape encloses the yin/yang symbol, and its eight sides represent the eight compass points, each of which governs a fundamental life issue: career, knowledge, health, wealth, fame, marriage, children, and benefactors. Each compass point includes other components—colors, seasons, numbers, and animals—within its sphere of influence. You can manipulate your fate through balanced and harmonious arrangement of these disparate items.

The four cardinal compass directions—south, west, north, and east—are affiliated with four of the five fundamental elements: fire, metal, water, and wood, respectively. The fifth element, earth, is at the center of the chart. In Chinese thought these five elements account for all matter and together they make up the essential life force: chi.

PUTTING FENG SHUI TO WORK

TO MAKE FENG SHUI WORK FOR YOU, IT'S IMPORTANT TO LOOK NOT JUST at your home and its furnishings but at your life circumstances and your goals in making changes in your life, whether personal or professional.

As you go through your home in each chapter, you'll be taking stock of these goals and finding directions, colors, elements, and other means to assist you in adjusting your chi for maximum benefit to your life. Before you begin applying a feng shui cure, you must make a correct diagnosis of your problem, and your goal.

Here are some tips to keep in mind:

- Focus. Spend some time thinking about yourself, your career, your family, your finances, your goals—in short, all the aspects of your life that you may wish to improve or change. (See exercise, page 10.)
- Be flexible. There may well be more than one cure for a situation, and some cures may work better or more quickly than others. Apply one and watch for results, however subtle. If you aren't seeing the desired results within a few weeks, apply a different method if it's practical to do so.

- Don't underestimate the power of slight changes. Depending on your goal and the room you're working with, adding a plant or mirror, hanging a certain picture, or moving a table to a different corner may be all that's needed.
- Be realistic. Remember that feng shui isn't magic. You'll be making subtle adjustments, and you must watch for subtle effects.
- Keep an open mind. As you monitor results, try to avoid either obsessively checking for results on a daily basis or, at the other extreme, cynically expecting no results at all. Balance is the key to feng shui.

It is comforting to know that with feng shui you are using time-tested methods for directing your destiny and influencing your fate. Three millennia of insight gleaned from careful observation is not a bad basis for arranging your home—and your life.

EXERCISE

HOW WELL FENG SHUI WORKS FOR YOU DEPENDS ON HOW CAREFULLY you focus on your personal goals. Take a few minutes to look over this list of questions and think deeply about your replies.

- Do you get up in the morning feeling refreshed, rested, and ready to go?
- Do any members of your family suffer from chronic health problems?
- Are you satisfied with your relationship with your spouse or partner?
- Does your family get along as well as you would like?
- Are you trying to have children?
- Is your job or career progressing as you would like it to?
- When you sit down to work at your desk, do you feel efficient, effective, and able to function well?

- Are you earning as much money as you think you should?
- Do you wish you had more control over your finances?
- Do you have good friends and helpful people in your life?
- Do your friends, colleagues, and family members think well of you?

Once you decide which aspects of your life you want to improve, you'll be more effective in selecting the areas in your home or office to concentrate on and the cures and enhancements that will work best for you. It is much better to work on just one or two issues at a time.

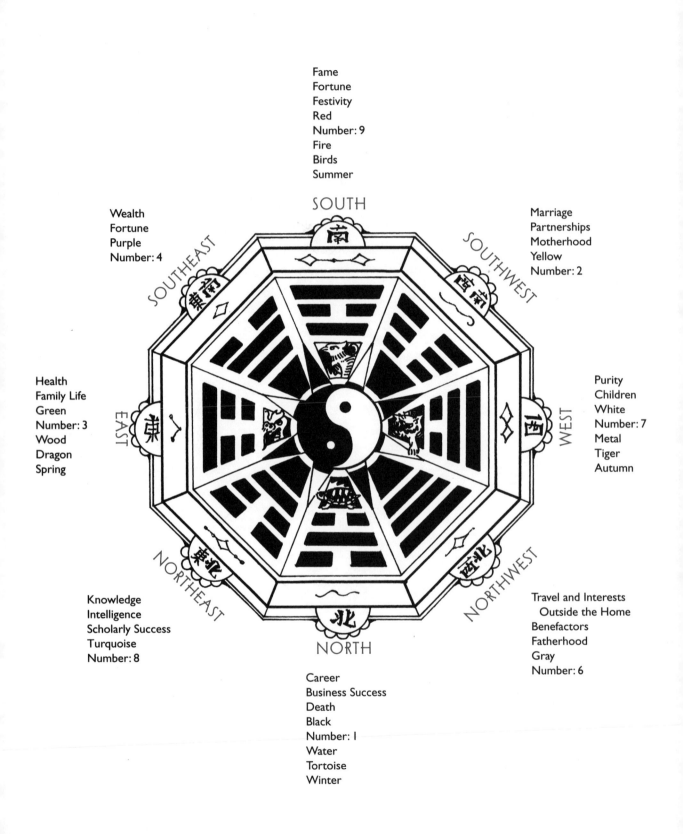

Fame
Fortune
Festivity
Red
Number: 9
Fire
Birds
Summer

SOUTH

Wealth
Fortune
Purple
Number: 4

SOUTHEAST

Marriage
Partnerships
Motherhood
Yellow
Number: 2

SOUTHWEST

Health
Family Life
Green
Number: 3
Wood
Dragon
Spring

EAST

WEST

Purity
Children
White
Number: 7
Metal
Tiger
Autumn

Knowledge
Intelligence
Scholarly Success
Turquoise
Number: 8

NORTHEAST

NORTHWEST

Travel and Interests
  Outside the Home
Benefactors
Fatherhood
Gray
Number: 6

NORTH

Career
Business Success
Death
Black
Number: 1
Water
Tortoise
Winter

TWO

BA-GUA BASICS

THE BASIC TOOLS OF FENG SHUI, THE MAJOR COMPONENTS OF THE BA-gua, come from the natural world around us: the directions of the compass; the five basic elements; and the colors of nature, from the fiery red of a sunset to the pale green of a new leaf. With careful use of these natural tools, you can achieve harmony with the environment and enjoy the health, happiness, and success that result.

THE EIGHT POINTS OF THE COMPASS ARE BASIC COMPONENTS OF FENG shui. With knowledge of these directions, their characteristics, and their spheres of influence, you can create good feng shui or make positive adjustments to remedy unfavorable situations.

THE COMPASS DIRECTIONS

THE CHINESE PLACE SO MUCH IMPORTANCE ON THE DIRECTION SOUTH that they put it at the top of their maps and navigate from it, in the same way that Westerners use north. (Note that the feng shui chart on

SOUTH

page 12 is laid out to reflect this, with south at the top.) South represents a high point in every sense of the word: just as it rules the top of the compass, it also represents summer, the "high noon" of the year. It is the most auspicious direction, and has many positive connotations. Fame, fortune, and festivity, thought to come most easily in the warm, leisurely days of summer, are all governed by the south. Not surprisingly, this direction is associated with heat, fire, and the color red, the color of celebration and happiness for the Chinese. If you paint a south-facing door red, you ward off harm while attracting fame and fortune. Birds are closely associated with south—think of the phoenix, eternally rising from the ashes to create itself anew, just as summer rises out of winter and day out of night. Nine, the largest single-digit number, suggesting the bounty of summer, is associated with the south.

WEST

THE DIRECTION OF THE SETTING SUN IS NATURALLY ASSOCIATED WITH autumn and with harvests. Metal, which is mined from the earth and is used to make plows, scythes, and other farming implements, is the corresponding element for this direction. The color of the west is white, representing the gleam of metal. The color white in turn suggests west's major spheres of influence, purity and children. The white tiger is the animal of the west; 7 is its number.

NORTH

AS THE SOUTH REPRESENTS THE HEAT, THE BOUNTY, AND THE ROSES OF summer, north is associated with cold temperatures, bleakness, and the blackness of deep winter. While the south is represented by fire, the north is linked to water, fire's opposing element. Water also symbolizes money in feng shui: the blacker or deeper the water, the more money is represented; the flow of water signifies cash flow. Careers and business are governed by this compass point. Some of the most negative aspects of life—death, calamity, and evil—fall under the north's sphere of influence. The north takes the tortoise, a symbol of longevity, as its animal, which mitigates the association with death. North's number is 1.

EAST, THE DIRECTION OF THE RISING SUN, IS THE COMPASS POINT associated with growth, health, and family life. Spring is the season associated with east, just as its opposite, autumn, is associated with west. Fittingly, youth and the color green are also under the domain of east. Wood, representing all growing things, is east's dominant element, and the dragon, symbolizing strength, power, and growth, is its animal. Harmony and prosperity are also governed by the east. Its number is 3.

HALF OF THE COMPASS POINTS GOVERN SOME ASPECT OF FINANCE, BUT the southeast is the compass point most directly associated with wealth. This may be because much of China's trade occurred in southeastern coastal cities; Hong Kong is a current example of a thriving southeastern trading center. Purple is the color primarily associated with this direction. Southeast is represented by the number 4.

ANOTHER COMPASS POINT WITH A VERY SPECIFIC PRACTICAL CONNOTATION, the southwest governs marriage, spouses, and partnerships of all kinds. It is also the direction of motherhood. Yellow—the color of that most basic of elements, earth—is southwest's predominant shade. Two—as in pairs, partners, and mother and child—is the number associated with this direction.

THIS IS THE DIRECTION TO PAY ATTENTION TO IF YOU OR SOMEONE IN your household has academic ambitions or is aiming for scholarly success. The northeast represents knowledge, intelligence, and learning. Turquoise is the color that corresponds to the northeast because it combines the sky blue of lofty aspirations with the green of growth and youth in the east. Eight, which sounds in Cantonese like the word for "to prosper," is the number of this direction because the Chinese put high stock in education as a means toward success and prosperity.

NORTHWEST

THE NORTHWEST AREAS OF YOUR HOME OR OFFICE HOLD SWAY OVER both domestic and international travel. This direction also governs fatherhood and major interests or hobbies that take place outside the home. One of the northwest's most powerful spheres of influence, reflecting life outside the family's walls, is benefactors, or helpful people. Six is the number of this compass point, and gray is its color.

THE FIVE ELEMENTS

ONE OF THE BEST WAYS TO CREATE GOOD FENG SHUI OR FIX BAD FENG shui is to make clever use of the five elements wherever possible in your home or office. Mixing, separating, and arranging the five elements at appropriate compass points is one of the basic methods of adjusting the feng shui in your home.

The elements interact in either a creative or a destructive cycle, and the manner in which they are represented in your home affects the delicate balance of your environment.

In the creative cycle, burning wood feeds fire; fire produces earth from its ashes; earth in turn gives up its ore, creating metal; metal brings forth water from condensation on its surface; and water nourishes and creates plants and trees, creating wood.

There is also a destructive cycle, which is reminiscent of the child's hand game "paper-scissors-rock": fire melts metal; metal cuts wood; wood decays into earth; earth muddies water; water quenches fire.

In ancient China, bad luck and natural disasters were thought to come from disruptions to the flow of the creative cycle. While you may not bring about calamities on a massive scale by disrupting the cycles, it's possible that you'll unwittingly upset parts of your personal and professional life by creating a destructive cycle. At the least, you

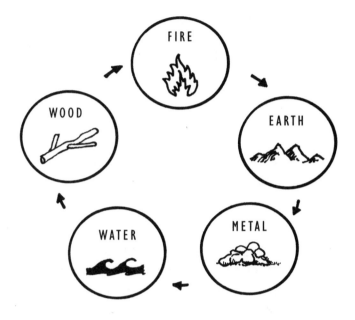

The creative cycle of
elements

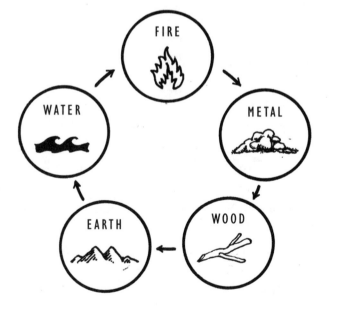

The destructive cycle of
elements

may be missing out on something positive by failing to use the creative cycle to your best advantage.

Here are some examples of creative and destructive combinations at work:

- Fire is associated with the direction south and the color red, as well as fame, fortune, and festivity. If you are trying to increase your fortune, achieve fame, or even just add a bit more festivity to your life, put some red candles in the south corner or wall of your living room or office.
- Water, on the other hand, puts fire out. Don't put an aquarium, a fountain, or even a picture of a body of water in the southern part of the room. Whether or not you are intentionally playing up the fire element in this area to enhance good fortune, placing water here will douse your chances of achieving fame, fortune, and other good things that the south has to offer.
- Avoid putting anything metal, such as brass candlesticks or pewter dishes or silverware, on an east wall. In the destructive cycle metal chops into wood, the east's element, and this could lead to disintegration of your family's strength or sense of cohesion.
- Since west is affiliated with children, you can help develop a young child's chi in a positive way by putting something white and metal (a lamp, a statue, a picture frame) on the west wall of his or her bedroom. Five-year-old Rory was being teased by his classmates until his parents strengthened his chi through a simple feng shui adjustment. Placing an ant farm with a white metal frame against the west wall of his room capitalized on Rory's interest in nature, while the use of dirt in the ant farm strengthened the positive effect, because in the creative cycle earth creates metal.

Have fun and be creative while you're building positive feng shui. Your goals and interests will lead you to the feng shui adjustments that are right for your individual requirements.

COLOR IS ONE OF THE MOST IMPORTANT ASPECTS OF ANY DECORATING scheme and is often the first thing you notice about a home. It can make a room seem larger or smaller, warmer or cooler, cheerful or bleak. Because color has such an effect on the feel as well as the look of a room, it is an important component in the feng shui of any room.

COLORS

The choice of color is also very personal. As you will see below, there is enough variation in the meaning and association of basic colors to give you plenty of leeway in selecting colors for good feng shui while still accommodating your taste.

Decorate a room in the shades that will enhance the activity, such as sleeping, studying, cooking, or entertaining, that will take place there. Or paint it with a color that corresponds to goals you hope to achieve in that room. For example, if you're just starting out in your own business and hope to achieve both success and a solid reputation, use the colors black, which signifies business success as well as money, and red, for fame, signifying your enhanced reputation, to decorate your office or study. While painting a study black would strike many as bleak and depressing to say the least, you can use black sparingly and still achieve an auspicious effect. Black accents in combination with lighter colors would be dramatic as well as favorable.

White is a color with dual associations. It is the color of purity, but also the color Chinese use for funerals and mourning; it is not used for weddings or other happy occasions as it is in the West. Use white where it's appropriate to signify purity—in a child's room or the kitchen. Because white is a yang color—yang corresponds to the masculine and has hardness and brightness among its qualities—you will want to offset a white room with touches of darker colors to add yin, a feminine, dark, soft element. This will keep the yin and yang of the room—and its feng shui—in balance. You should avoid decorating the living room all in white. Because the living room is the most public place in your home, it's already a yang room. An all-white living room would be a hard and sterile place, not at all conducive to relaxation or friendly get-togethers.

Both green and blue are associated with the element wood, with spring and new beginnings. The ancient Chinese used the same word to describe the blue of the sky or the green of growing things. Both colors are especially appropriate for east-facing rooms, where they enhance health, family life, harmony, and growth.

Yellow is useful and versatile in the home. It was the official color of the emperors, and it can be used today to add a touch of nobility to any room. Select tones from the palest yellows to the deepest tans or golds for your family room, your office, or wherever you would like to attract brightness or great honor. Yellow also corresponds to the southwest, which governs motherhood; the color is frequently used to good effect in the bedroom of couples hoping to have a child.

> The Chinese word for yellow, *huang,* sounds like the word for "royal." That's why this color was selected thousands of years ago as the exclusive color for the imperial household. Under pain of death, no Chinese person except the emperor was permitted to wear any shade of yellow or gold. Because the emperor embodied the link between heaven and earth, yellow is sometimes used in feng shui to symbolize that connection, enhancing the yin/yang balance of a room. Today yellow is also thought to bring nobility and high honors, especially to a family.

Red is *the* lucky color. It is associated with fire, life, happiness, and warmth. At Chinese New Year, employees and children in Chinese families are given little red packets or envelopes filled with money or treats as symbols of good wishes. Chinese brides wear red dresses, and birthday cards and wedding invitations are printed on red paper. Red is associated with the direction south. If you're lucky enough to have a front door or gate that faces this way, by all means paint it red!

NOT ALL NUMBERS ARE CREATED EQUAL. SOME ARE MUCH MORE AUSPI- **NUMBERS**
cious than others and are highly coveted for addresses, telephone and fax numbers, and license plates.

Nine represents the fullness of heaven and earth. It is the luckiest of all numbers, in part because of its apparently mystical qualities: when you multiply 9 by any single-digit number, the sum of the two digits of the product is 9. For example, 2 times 9 equals 18—and 1 plus 8 makes nine. Seven times 9 equals 63, and 3 plus 6 makes 9. It's no coincidence that 9 is also the number associated with south, the most auspicious direction in feng shui.

The feng shui expert Lillian Too tells the story of the Hong Kong magnate Dickson Poon, who swears by 9's special qualities. To ensure his good luck, Poon's personal Rolls-Royce sports a license plate with the number 9999.

The number 8 is another favorite, owing to the similarity of its pronunciation to the Cantonese word for "prosperity." Other numbers with 8 in them are also lucky because of the way they sound in Cantonese. Forty-eight, for example, sounds like "much prosperity." Twenty-eight's popularity stems from its sounding like "easy prosperity." Fifty-eight, on the other hand, is avoided because it sounds like "no prosperity."

The Cantonese word for 6 sounds like the word for "deer." This animal is a symbol of long life, so 6 is considered a lucky number.

Four is at the top of the list of bad-luck numbers because it is pronounced "si," which sounds just like the word for death. One prospective home buyer in California refused to enter a house with the address 444. When his realtor asked why he wouldn't even go inside and look around, the man replied, "Why would I want to live in a house that says, 'Die, die, die'?" There are ways, however, to use this number to your advantage. You can enhance the wealth-giving properties of the southeast by placing four purple objects, such as flowers or artwork, in the southeastern area of your home or room, because 4 and purple are this direction's corresponding number and color.

T H R E E

YOUR HOME IN
THE WORLD

THE CIRCULATION OF CHI IN YOUR BODY AND AROUND YOUR HOME HAS a tremendous impact on your life. Chi is everywhere, but it can exist in forms that are either beneficial or harmful, depending on its flow and speed. Free-flowing chi that circulates smoothly has a positive influence, bringing vital energy to everything in its path. Chi that is blocked and becomes stagnant, or chi that moves too rapidly, can have a negative effect on your well-being. Harnessing good chi and directing its flow is in large part the goal of feng shui.

Once you understand how to attract good chi, you can manipulate its flow in ways that allow you to enjoy its benefits and attain specific goals. And when you know what causes bad chi, you will also be able to correct problems by "repairing" flow patterns that are creating difficulties in your own or your family's life.

Chi is a force of nature, the breath of life. Where the natural world is thriving, or where the patterns of nature are echoed indoors, chi will thrive. In turn, where chi flows smoothly, the balance of nature will be clear.

Look around your neighborhood to assess the way chi may be affecting you. Healthy grass, trees, and landscaping, neatly kept yards, and well-maintained houses or apartment buildings are a fairly reliable indication that chi is flowing nicely and that yin and yang are in balance. Brown grass, stunted trees, or dilapidated buildings may indicate that chi is moving too rapidly or perhaps is blocked or stagnant.

Good neighbors are another indication that positive chi is flowing in your area. Being surrounded by friendly and helpful people is just one of the benefits of healthy chi. Good neighbors not only reflect good chi but also help perpetuate it by providing assistance and protection to one another, whether lending the occasional egg or cup of sugar, or keeping a concerned eye on one another's property to help prevent crime.

If what you see around you does not look good and feel positive, do not despair. There are various adjustments you can make to improve this flow of chi, from fixing up your own house and yard as much as possible to other measures for creating vibrant, smooth-flowing chi outside your home. You don't need hills or a meandering stream on your property to assist in chi flow. There are ways to symbolically gain the advantages that these natural elements provide.

DRAGONS AND TIGERS

CHINA'S MOST FAMOUS LANDMARK, THE GREAT WALL, IS AN IMPRESSIVE fortress meandering through miles of mountain terrain. One look makes it clear how important protection has always been in Chinese thought. The best protection, according to the ancient Land Form School of feng shui, comes from tigers and dragons—not the fire breathers of Western mythology, but the benevolent protectors of Chinese lore. When you recall that the Chinese consider chi the cosmic breath of the celestial dragon, you'll understand why you'd want to have a dragon near your home.

Of course, even in ancient China, dragons and tigers weren't common house pets! The dragons and tigers in question are actually hills and mountains arranged in a particular way for maximum protection and good feng shui.

According to the venerable Land Form School, the perfect location for your home would have a "green dragon" hill to the east, a "white tiger" slope to the west, and a range of hills symbolizing the "black tortoise" to your back. These colors correspond to the compass point each animal represents on the ba-gua chart. Green represents the east, white is the color of the west, and black is associated with the north.

This position among protective land masses effectively nestles your home in a geological armchair, with a high back and protective sides, suggesting comfort as well as the natural guardianship afforded by the mythical beasts. For perfect balance, the strong protective dragon, representing the masculine yang element, is paired with the tiger, which represents the feminine, or yin, aspect of the universe. In addition to the protection and harmony of the tiger and dragon on either side, the tortoise at your back bestows the added benefit of longevity that this animal symbolizes.

Of course, in many modern neighborhoods, living under the benevolent protection of dragons and tigers—or even hills—is difficult. But the symbolic guardianship of the dragon and the tiger can be yours through other means.

Ideal home position between dragon and tiger hills

Large shady backyard trees or any slightly larger buildings to your home's back and sides can stand in for the "armchair" hills. And just as you cultivate the trees for protection, you should also cultivate your neighbors. Good neighbors are among the most important guardians for the contemporary home, and they make an excellent substitute for the dragon and tiger.

POISON ARROWS

WINDING OR GENTLY MEANDERING CURVES REFLECT NATURE'S DESIGN, whereas straight lines are considered unnatural in feng shui because they usually indicate tampering with the natural surroundings. These straight lines are a frequent cause of high-velocity chi that can be dangerous to health and well-being. Chi directed by buildings or other structures along straight lines or shaped by sharp angles forms what is known as secret or poison arrows. When these arrows point at you or your property, you are vulnerable to their destructive energies.

Here are some sources of poison arrows to watch for around your building, street, and yard:

- Telephone poles or streetlights directly outside your door
- Angled roof lines that point toward your home
- Jutting corners of other buildings that point like arrows in your direction

If you have a poison arrow aimed at your home, block it with a tree or hedge, or deflect it with an exterior mirror aimed toward the source of the arrow.

THE FRONT DOOR

YOUR FRONT DOOR IS THE GATEWAY NOT JUST TO THE INTERIOR OF YOUR home, but to your personal life; it's a conduit from the outside world, giving visitors their first impression of you as well as of the place where you live. This door and the approach to it are critical factors in the feng shui of your entire home. Think of the front door as a valve for chi—it can attract healthy chi or it can allow negative forces to surround you and your family.

Ideally, the walkway to your front door should curve slightly, making an inviting path. At worst, a straight path may be a source of poison arrows aimed at your door; at best, the direct line will not be conducive to an optimum flow of chi through your main entry. If you do have a straight path to your door, place bricks, attractive stones, or potted plants at various points along the edge of the walk to break up the straightness of the line.

The size of your front door should be in proportion to the over-all size of your home. Too large a door can let valuable chi out, while a narrow door won't let enough good chi in. Feng shui practitioners from the old school say that the front door should face south, toward the warmth of the sun and the aspect that captures fame, fortune, and longevity. Of course, it's not practical, or even possible, for all doors to face this way. But luckily there are other ways to ensure that positive chi flows through your front door.

Positive chi is always attracted to bright, welcoming entryways. Your door should be attractive and in good repair and there should be no untidiness on the porch or path to the door; a weathered door with peeling paint is definitely a sign of bad feng shui. Signs of decay and disrepair discourage good chi and tend to encourage the negative energy of sha, or noxious chi. Good light is also critical to good chi; burned-out porch lights should immediately be replaced. If you don't have an outside light, install one and keep it lit in the evening, whether you are at home or away.

The front door should not open directly toward a church, temple, or cemetery because the yin coming from any of these is too strong. Yin is passive, dark, and cold with associations of death; too much yin directed at your home will make it a lonely and depressing place.

It is also bad luck to face a narrow gap between two buildings.

Mirrors can be used both inside and outside to draw auspicious views into the home. For instance, if you live close to a good source of chi—an ocean or lake or scenic mountain range—a mirror placed to reflect the source can draw that image and its positive influences to you.

Concave mirrors, which produce an inverted image, are used to defy sha, or bad chi, and send it in another direction. You may have noticed small octagonal, or ba-gua-shaped, mirrors hanging in Chinese restaurants or on the outside of buildings in Chinatown. These auspiciously shaped mirrors deflect evil influences and are generally reserved for the most serious sha threats.

A T-shaped intersection allows chi to flow too quickly toward your home.

In general, signs of life and movement attract good chi. If you are away from home a lot, leave the radio on, or hang wind chimes that tinkle in the breeze. Healthy plants or a bubbling aquarium, properly placed, will also encourage good chi in an empty house or apartment.

The gap can create a reverse poison arrow, sucking healthy chi away from your doorway and your home. Plant a large shrub or tree near the front door to cover these unlucky views and the forces they encourage.

Your home's location on the street can affect the flow of positive or negative chi toward it. It's bad feng shui to have your door open on to the junction of a T in the roadway or the dead-end of a street. There are practical reasons why this might be a problem: headlights may shine in your windows at night and accidents may occur more readily at odd intersections. But the chief culprit is the straight line that channels chi too quickly toward your door. If your home is situated at a T junction, plant shrubs or build a wall to keep this negative energy from propelling itself into your front door. You can even put a small mirror on the front of the building to deflect those noxious forces. The gentle movement of a weathervane on your roof will also help correct the problem by dispersing the bad chi or sha as it hurtles toward the house.

Steps leading up to your door should not be too steep or narrow. If you have steep, narrow stairs, put a mirror at the landing or above the door to open up the view and widen the approach.

Your front door also should not be at the foot of steps that lead down to it. If your house is located below street level, the chi can be trapped, unable to get up and out. Trapped chi frequently causes business or career difficulties because it keeps vital energy inside the house, instead of allowing it to flow from you out into the world. Installing a spotlight aimed up at the roof will correct this problem.

By the same token, a downward slope at the rear of your building is undesirable, because it allows chi, good luck, and wealth to slip away from you. A weathervane on the roof, a spotlight pointing toward the roof, or even a tree that comes nearly to the roofline will help lift this dragging chi.

Obstructions at or near the door also indicate bad feng shui because they can block good chi, prosperity, and luck from entering your home. Any of these obstructions should be paid attention to:

- A single tree directly outside your front door
- A retaining wall right outside your door
- A hill or mound that obstructs the approach to the front door

You don't need to cut down a tree or demolish a wall or hill if you have any of these situations. The quickest remedy is to suspend a crystal or wind chimes on or as close as possible to the obstruction. The multifaceted surface of the crystal will capture and radiate the chi. The gentle movement and soothing sounds of the wind chimes will encourage its optimum circulation.

If you like, you can provide guards for your home by flanking your entryway with urns of plants or flowers, or even the whimsical touch of symbolic sentinels such as Chinese Fu dogs on either side of the door.

INSIDE THE ENTRY

WHEN YOU STEP INSIDE YOUR HOME, YOU SHOULD ENTER A CHEERFUL, roomy, and well-lit area that immediately welcomes you and your guests. Dark and narrow foyers or entry halls hinder the flow of chi and are highly undesirable. It's preferable not to face another wall as soon as you enter, as this, too, can block the chi flow and can create obstructions everywhere you turn in life. You can fix these defects easily enough. Install soft, warm lighting if the entryway is dark. Hang a picture on a wall directly opposite the door—preferably of a landscape or other open vista—to open up this constricted area.

Some feng shui masters prescribe a mirror to open and brighten the entry. Other practitioners caution that confronting your guests with an immediate and unexpected image of themselves as they walk through your door could startle or upset any but the vainest visitors.

The decision for your home should be based on whatever you are most comfortable with.

STAIRCASES AND DOORS

STAIRCASES ARE IMPORTANT BECAUSE THEY CONDUCT CHI FROM ONE floor to another. An interior staircase should never directly face the front door because chi, good luck, and money can run right down the staircase—out the door and out of your life. Ideally, the stairs should curve gently upward. Mirrors are a frequently used "cure" for poor staircase and door alignment. A mirror on the landing of a staircase will draw the chi in and reflect it back out around the interior, preventing it from departing too quickly through the door.

It is undesirable to have your back door directly visible from the front entrance. In this arrangement, the chi will flow too quickly in the front door and out the back and won't circulate beneficially throughout your home. Many U.S. builders and developers who sell to an Asian clientele have stopped building homes with this door alignment because they are classic examples of bad feng shui. It is also considered unlucky to have a clear view from the front door straight through your home and into the backyard. This arrangement can allow good luck and prosperity to rush in and out again without stopping. Furthermore, the Chinese believe that showing guests the back exit the minute they walk in the front door is not very hospitable!

Three doors in alignment is also considered very bad feng shui, and it's especially unlucky if one door is a front entrance and the other is the rear exit. There are various remedies you can use. Folding screens, a tall plant, or beaded curtains will block the sha from this alignment. You may prefer to suspend a crystal, which will attract good chi while it disperses sha; or you can hang a pair of bamboo flutes above the middle opening, which will draw the sha up and out while it makes the inauspicious arrangement "disappear" symbolically.

To correct the inauspicious alignment of front and back doors, suspend wind chimes or a crystal pendant from the ceiling just inside the front door. The gentle movement of the chimes and the brilliant facets of the crystal capture and redistribute the chi as a positive force. You might even want to place a folding screen or other partial barrier to interfere with the direct channel from front to back, or to block a view through to the backyard.

THE SHAPE OF YOUR HOUSE OR APARTMENT BUILDING ALSO AFFECTS the feng shui of your living space. Square or rectangular homes are thought to be most auspicious because they are self-contained areas that leave no rooms "dangling" outside the main floor plan. Feng shui practitioners advise against irregularly shaped homes because harm can come to those living in the "odd" areas. The occupant of a dangling room will be cut off from the normal interaction of the household, leading to difficulties ranging from poor study habits and minor health complaints to more serious misfortunes. This person is cut off from the protection of the family and is also out of the path of beneficial chi circulation.

THE SHAPE OF YOUR HOME

In particular, an L-shaped home or room is inauspicious. The asymmetrical L shape suggests an incomplete rectangle, and thus the quality of incompleteness; the building is out of balance, with some crucial element missing. Harmony and balance are the ideal in feng shui, and symmetrical shapes reflect these qualities.

An L shape also suggests a meat cleaver, the long wall standing for the handle and the shorter section, the blade. This rather brutal image can have negative effects for the person who resides near the "blade." In a cleaver-shaped room or part of the house, avoid putting a bed, stove, or desk at the blade edge. Try to avoid using the cleaver-shaped portion of a house as a family member's bedroom. Anyone who must regularly sleep or work in a blade area will be accident-prone, nervous, and jumpy. If it's impossible to avoid placing impor-

Fill in the "missing" piece of an L-shaped building for improved feng shui.

tant furniture such as a bed, stove, or desk against the blade edge, hang a mirror above the piece of furniture to draw it away from the cutting edge into the relative safety of the room.

To correct the imbalance of an L-shaped home, put a tree, a flagpole, or even a spotlight in the open space to complete the rectangle. You can use this method to "fill out" any other irregularly shaped buildings.

AND KEEP IN MIND . . .

IN GENERAL, THE AIMS OF THE FENG SHUI MASTER AND THE ARCHITECT are the same. Both want to ensure that your home and the rooms within it are designed to function well for their intended purpose and to promote good chi flow, which the architect calls air circulation. The building should also encourage harmony and balance in the lives of the inhabitants by providing sufficient public and private spaces. In feng shui, the all-important goal of balance is also achieved through careful attention to every room, with appropriate decoration and arrangement according to the activities that will take place in it. Whether you are sleeping, working, cooking, reading, socializing, or eating, you should be in harmony with your surroundings.

FOUR

THE BEDROOM

ACCORDING TO THE TENETS OF FENG SHUI, THE BEDROOM IS THE MOST important room because where and how you sleep exerts a major influence on your life. If your bedroom inspires tranquil feelings and leads you to peacefulness and proper rest, you will reap the benefits in a multitude of ways. Sex, wealth, health, and the happiness of a marriage can all be enhanced by a bedroom with good feng shui.

You spend fully one third of your life in the bedroom, whether sleeping, reading, making love, or just retreating into the kind of privacy that no other room can afford. When you lie in bed, you're doing more than resting—you are literally gaining the strength and the spiritual refreshment needed to go out into the world and carry on with the rest of your life.

You want the room to reflect your true spirit. The bedroom is—or should be—the most personal room in your home and the one in which you feel safest and most comfortable. Consider how vulnerable you are in here. You're asleep, unaware of anything taking place around you; you're generally undressed and unprotected by even so much as a pair of shoes.

According to Chinese thought, the soul leaves the body while we sleep to wander and restore itself in the astral plane, which most people in the Western world think of as dreaming. However you think of it, you know that while your conscious mind has the night off, the all-important subconscious is busy at work, recreating and reordering feelings, memory, and experience for the benefit of your psyche.

Because the delicate interplay between your conscious and subconscious mind is so crucial to your ability to function well, you will want to arrange and decorate your bedroom with utmost care, paying attention to feng shui principles as closely as possible. When you do, you will reap the maximum in benefits from this important room.

BED PLACEMENT

IF YOUR BED IS PLACED INAUSPICIOUSLY, YOU WILL FEEL OFF BALANCE, whether awake or asleep, because the chi in the room will be seriously disturbed. Finding the best spot for your bed is the first task.

The main rule of bed placement is never to have the foot of your bed in direct alignment with the door. In ancient China and many other cultures, the dead were laid out with their feet pointing out the door to allow them easier access to heaven—and, not incidentally, to make it easier for the living to carry them out. This arrangement came to be known as the "death position"—more rest than any of us want when we retire for the night.

Chi should be able to flow unobstructed from the door through the room, so it is important that the bed not block the path of chi through a doorway. Also, having your head in line with the door can make you restless and vulnerable to the surprise of an unexpected visitor. Sleeping in view of the door is all right, as long as your head is some distance from it.

Ideally, the bed should be placed diagonally opposite the room's

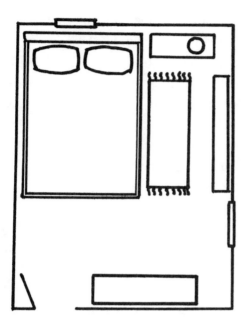

The "death position" for bed placement

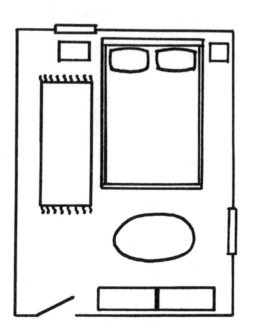

Ideal position for bed placement

main entrance. This will allow for the best flow of energy in the room and keep you from the drafts, interruptions, and distractions in the door's path.

You should try to put the bed against a solid wall, not a window. If putting it against a window is unavoidable, leave a small gap, enough for a chair or table, between the bed and window. Chi can escape from windows at night, and you don't want the precious chi force that flows through your body to be depleted while you're asleep. Make sure you cover any bedroom windows at night to further slow the flight of environmental chi.

The feng shui master Johndennis Govert recommends locating your bed so that your head points north, as long as you can do so without violating any of the principles for auspicious bed placement. This north-south alignment ensures that your body's axis is parallel to the earth's and will be in a direct line to receive the magnetic energy that enters the earth at the North Pole. The direct path to your brain of this vital force will enable you to remember your dreams and enhance your perceptions and understanding of them.

Never place a bed under a low slanting ceiling or under exposed beams. These angular protrusions are carriers of sha and can cause headaches, illness, confused thinking, and even financial and career problems. An exposed beam that runs the length of the bed can cause marital discord between the sleepers if they are divided by the beam. Beams that run horizontally over the bed can create aches, pains, and diseases in the parts of the body routinely exposed to their negative energy. In the worst case, horizontal beams can literally "cut in half" the life of the sleeper.

MIRRORS AND BEDROOM FURNITURE

MIRRORS IN THE BEDROOM SHOULD NEVER FACE THE BED. WHEN THE sleeper's spirit rises at night it will get a nasty shock coming face to face with its own image, which can be very disturbing to the serenity of the sleeper. In fact, while mirrors are used frequently with very positive results throughout the rest of the home, feng shui tenets dictate a sparing use of them in the bedroom. One mirror—one that does not reflect the bed—is the maximum prescribed for this part of the house.

Bookcases, dressers, and other bedroom furniture should not be placed so that their sharp edges point toward the sleeper in the bed. The energy coming off the two planes that create the corner is dangerously fast and sharp. This constant bombardment with pointing rays of energy can be harmful to your health; at the very least, it may cause irritability.

BEDROOM SHAPE

AS WITH THE SHAPE OF YOUR HOME, REGULAR SHAPES ARE CONSIDERED best for the rooms, including the bedroom. Square or rectangular rooms allow for maximum chi flow, while irregular shapes can block chi. An irregularly shaped bedroom may have corners that jut out, creating poison arrows. Anyone regularly exposed to these arrows, especially while sleeping, can suffer ill effects in the form of minor health problems, mood swings, and loss of concentration.

For optimal chi flow the bedroom ceiling should be neither too high nor too low. Cathedral ceilings, which also often have exposed beams, are considered too high, and anything less than the standard eight-foot ceiling of a contemporary American home is too low.

LOCATION IN THE HOME

THE SOUTHWEST AREA OF YOUR DWELLING IS THE IDEAL PLACE TO locate the master bedroom. This direction governs marriage, spouses, and partnerships. If you have the choice, your bedroom should be located toward the rear of your house or apartment, as far away from the noise of the street and the hubbub of family activities as possible.

A child or student's bedroom situated in the northeast part of the home will be very conducive to his or her scholarly success because this compass point governs knowledge and academic achievement.

CLUTTER AND
ELECTRONIC
EQUIPMENT

If you have a chronically cluttered spot in your home— and who doesn't?—hang a crystal ball above it. This will get the chi moving more quickly and lessen the area's tendency to be a dumping ground.

USING YOUR BEDROOM AS A STORAGE AREA FOR BOXES, SPARE FURNI-
ture, or stacks of books and paper will block the smooth flow of chi in
the room and around your bed. This interrupted chi flow can make
you feel jumpy and disturb your sleep. Storing junk under your bed
will cause chi to stagnate there. Because the bed is the basis of good
health as well as marital harmony, sleeping over stagnant chi can
cause problems in these areas of your life.

Master Govert cautions against keeping electronic equipment,
such as televisions, radios, stereos, or computers, in the bedroom. The
electromagnetic field of these appliances cancels out any benefits of
north-south alignment you may have achieved from careful bed
placement, interfering with your ability to remember and understand
your dreams. He also advises that fireplaces, wet bars, and other
amenities common to modern master bedroom suites are detrimental
to the tranquillity of the room. If there is a television set in the bedroom, he recommends placing an opaque cloth over the screen
before retiring for the night because it may act as a mirror in the room
and disturb your spirit while you sleep.

FIXES

THE PRECEDING RECOMMENDATIONS MAY LEAVE YOU CLUTCHING YOUR
head in despair of arranging your bedroom in any way that doesn't
pose at least one feng shui dilemma. In many bedrooms, just squeez-
ing in the bed and a dresser is tricky, let alone placing them in auspicious positions!

Luckily, there are several ways you can not only "fix" bad feng
shui but also enhance the room so that it helps you meet your goals
and aspirations.

If you can't avoid having the foot of your bed pointed toward the
door, or having your bed in the path of the doorway, hang a crystal
sphere or wind chimes from the ceiling between the bed and the

entrance to disperse the sha and lessen its adverse affects. If there's space, you might even want to put up a folding screen, blocking the direct path between the bed and door.

If exposed beams or a sloping ceiling menace your sleep, hang two bamboo flutes pointing upward on the offending protrusion. Because the word for "flute" in Cantonese sounds the same as the word for "disappear," the suspended instruments will make the beams disappear—symbolically.

The dangers of sharp-cornered furniture and jutting walls that aim poison arrows at your bed can be corrected by hanging a crystal from the ceiling or placing a plant or folding screen between them. Either of these objects will slow the flow of chi to a safe place.

ENHANCEMENTS

AS YOU CONSIDER THE ARRANGEMENT AND DECORATION OF YOUR BED-room, think again about the ambitions and goals you outlined for yourself in Chapter 1. Special enhancements in your bedroom or the bedroom of a family member can help you achieve these personal wishes.

Enhancing the northeast corner of a child's or student's bed-room can promote his or her academic success. Green-blue is the color that corresponds to the northeast direction, so you may want to paint the room a not-too-vibrant shade of turquoise. Primary colors are fine for a child's room, unless he or she tends to be hyperactive or otherwise has trouble sleeping, in which case soothing pastel tones are more appropriate. You can further enhance this room with the number 8, since it corresponds to the northeast. Eight bright blue-and-green nature scenes mounted on the wall will fascinate your child, beautify the room, and create a powerful enhancement that incorporates both colors and numbers.

If your "home office" is in reality a corner of your bedroom, you

At thirty-nine Anne Marie had been happily married to Walt for ten years, but she was beginning to feel frantic about not being able to get pregnant. The couple had good jobs, a large home in a nice part of town, and supportive friends; in every other way they felt their life was going well. At a party one evening, Anne Marie told a Chinese friend that she was ready to try anything if only she could have a baby. Her friend asked if Anne Marie knew anything about feng shui. Anne Marie said that she didn't but would be interested to learn.

The feng shui master that the couple eventually called into their home went straight to the bedroom. At his suggestion, they moved their bed to the southwest corner of the room, the direction that governs both marriage and motherhood. Next, they painted the room yellow to correspond to the color of the southwest. On the west wall, which governs children, they hung a grouping of seven pictures in white frames, because seven is the number and white the color of this direction. To touch on as many auspicious symbols as possible, they even bought a large stuffed tiger, the animal that Chinese mythology places in the west, and propped it against the wall. Now the cuddly animal sits in the crib of their son, Gus, who was born about a year later.

might want to maximize your intellectual abilities by putting the desk in the northeast section of the room. On the other hand, you might prefer to work with your desk positioned against the north wall because north is the direction that directly influences business success. See Chapter 7 for more on the application of feng shui principles in the office.

It is most auspicious, as well as most pleasing, to face an attractive view when you awaken. We can't all look out on views of the Pacific Ocean or the Berkshires, but we can do our best to make sure that our eyes fall on pleasant things—art, plants, attractive draperies, even favorite books—when we open our eyes in the morning.

And when we close them, we can hardly do better than to meditate on our goals and aspirations. In feng shui, conscious intent is important to the achievement of your goals and meditating on them is an excellent way to focus that intent. Jot down just a couple of your aspirations and keep the paper near your bedside so your notes are handy to look at before you turn out the light. You'll be making use of a perfect opportunity to literally help your dreams come true.

FIVE

THE LIVING ROOM AND DINING ROOM

HOW YOU HANDLE THE ARRANGEMENT AND DECORATION OF YOUR LIV-
ing room will affect many critical aspects of your life, from friendships
and family relationships to success and prosperity.

The living room or family room is the most lively and public
place inside your home. Its look and feel will tell visitors many things
about you and your family. The furniture, carpet, and general decor
might suggest something about your social life or financial status,
whereas the room's ambience tells the world a thing or two about
your personality.

Your choice of furniture and the way you group it may declare
that you are a casual, fun-loving family, or a formal one; it may reflect
a very traditional disposition, or a highly contemporary viewpoint.
The artwork and family treasures you display in this room will reveal
your aspirations as well as your accomplishments.

Whatever your taste and style preference, your goal should be to
create a serene and welcoming effect. This is critical because more

than any other room in your home, your living room governs the kind of people you attract. Friends, relatives, and visitors will respond to the atmosphere you create for them here.

Your immediate family also responds to the feelings evoked by the living or family room. If it is not a cozy and welcoming spot, family members may find other places to spend their time. If chi is not flowing through the room in a vibrant and healthy way, family relationships will be disrupted and the family structure itself can suffer.

The Osgood family living room could have been photographed for an architectural magazine. With its starkly modern furniture, minimalist color scheme, and bold modern art pieces, the room was definitely a showplace. The problem was, none of the family ever felt like spending time there and the Osgoods had done little entertaining in it because they'd had no luck making friends in their new neighborhood.

Mrs. Osgood had done the decorating herself and was proud of it. But after several months of feeling that their living room had become a kind of no-man's-land, she began to see it as a depressing place. A month or so later she read an article about feng shui and called in a feng shui practitioner, who was able to point out several things that were causing problems.

The room faced east, which offered an ideal starting point for a living room, since east governs family life, youth, prosperity, and harmony. But because east is affiliated with the element wood, a large metal sculpture on the east wall was cutting into these aspects rather than enhancing them. (Metal cuts wood in the destructive cycle of elements.) The room was further plagued by its color scheme of beige, cream, and brown. Chi was being drained right out of the room by the lack of color. Moreover, the beige and cream shades were very close to white, which in Chinese culture is the color of mourning. Such pale shades are not prohibited, but they should be used sparingly, and preferably with bright accents to counter any suggestion of death and funerals.

By replacing the metal sculpture with a healthy indoor tree, the Osgoods accomplished several things at once. Suddenly their family life and harmony were being enhanced by the color green and the element wood. Adding other touches of color to the room, such as a set of vivid red throw pillows on a pair of chairs and artwork featuring nine brilliant red cardinals on the south wall, increased the family's interest in entertaining and their friendships in the neighborhood. Red was chosen because it corresponds with the direction south, the compass point that governs festivity and fame. (Here, "fame" is interpreted simply as reputation, or getting acquainted with new people.) The splashes of red also added much-needed warmth to the room, which the Osgoods were soon using for both family and neighborhood gatherings.

THE LIVING ROOM AND FAMILY GOALS

ALTHOUGH THE SOUTHEAST AREA OF ANY ROOM IN YOUR HOME GOVERNS your prospects for wealth, the southeast portion of your living room contains the most powerful and important wealth sector. The general bustle of the room makes the flow of chi very strong, and that powerful chi can have a dramatic effect when it flows through the room's wealth area.

Keep in mind that "wealth" doesn't always signify money. In the living room or family room, "wealth" can refer to whatever the family's primary interest, chief enthusiasm, or main focus may be. Perhaps the family's "wealth" is an abundance of good friends and an active social life. Perhaps it's an enthusiasm for camping and the outdoors. Or maybe business and academic success are at the heart of the family's passions. Whatever it is that absorbs the attention of the group, this aspect of life will be influenced by your wealth corner.

As in other aspects of feng shui, it is important to know oneself—and one's family—in order to make the wealth corner work for you. What are the goals of the household? If your family is hoping for a major excursion, such as a trip across the country or to Europe, then

Good lighting equals good chi. Dark rooms and buildings are almost always negative. If you have a problem area and aren't sure what to do to improve it, bright but not harsh light is a good choice.

activate the southeast corner by drawing in some of the symbols from the northwest, which governs trips and international travel as well as interests outside the home. Notice on the chart that the color gray and the number 6 belong to the northwest. Use your imagination to decorate your "wealth corner" in ways that will enhance your prospects of making the trip and help it to be a successful one for everyone in the household.

If the family's goal is to move to a larger house, by all means play up the wealth corner to attract money. A tank with four fish would use the southeast's number in combination with water and fish, which are symbols for cash flow and abundance. For any family goal that requires a bigger bank account, try incorporating purple, the southeast's color. Use your imagination to add touches of this fortune-enhancing shade while maintaining your decorating scheme. Clever ideas might include plants, which can be doubly effective if they burst forth with purple blossoms. An African violet, or even a bouquet of four irises, would be an excellent choice.

FURNITURE ARRANGEMENT

THE PLACEMENT OF YOUR LIVING-ROOM SOFA, COFFEE TABLE, AND chairs can either encourage warmth and sharing among guests or create situations where there is discord and friction. For example, guests seated in facing chairs with nothing between them may feel contrary toward one another and disagree on many issues. But if there is a shared table between them, they are likely to feel they have more in common and be kindly disposed toward one another. This arrangement also makes sense in terms of comfort and hospitality.

You should arrange seating so that the host and hostess will not have their backs to doors or windows while entertaining. Hosts should have the support of solid walls so that they will extend their hospitality with strength and power and also feel secure enough to be gracious.

If your living room can accommodate it, it is considered auspicious to arrange furniture so that it simulates the ba-gua. Of course, the octagon is a lucky shape because of its association with the ba-gua, but it is also a desirable figure because it has no right angles and is self-contained.

In the living room—as in every room—envision the flow of chi as you arrange the room's contents. Chi should progress gently; it moves best when it is allowed to flow unobstructed around furniture groupings. It should be encouraged to meander slowly, making its way from the entry door and touching on each area of the room before leaving through a door or window.

Don't forget that your front door is an important valve for chi. If the door is well proportioned in relation to the exterior of the house as well as to the room it opens on, you will be getting a good supply of chi. You won't want to block it by obstructing its path with furniture. You would want to avoid, for example, placing a sofa or table in the path of the door if it creates a barrier that chi, as well as your family and guests, must move around to get into the house.

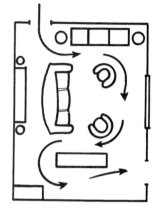

Arrange furniture to enhance a gentle flow of chi.

THE LIVING ROOM SHOULD BE CLOSE TO THE FRONT DOOR AND SHOULD be on the same level, not sunken. If you have a sunken living room, shine a bright light upward toward the ceiling. This will raise the chi, which otherwise will not be able to rise and move around the room properly.

If your living room is L-shaped, use a folding screen or an arrangement of plants to create distinct sitting areas and arrange the furniture in separate conversational groups. That way, you will have two rooms rather than one room with a dangling appendage or knife blade at one end.

Sofas and chairs should never be placed under overhanging beams because these constructions are oppressive to those seated beneath. If you can't avoid this arrangement, a pair of hollow bamboo

SHAPE AND PLACEMENT OF THE LIVING ROOM

flutes hung from the beam will make the problem "disappear" symbolically. At the same time, the round hollowness of the flute conducts the chi past the offending beam and mitigates its negative effect.

Because the living room is the most public room in the house, it's especially auspicious if yours faces south, the direction governing fame and fortune, festivity, and longevity. The other directions are not bad, though—just less favorable. Any compass point should provide an opportunity to move toward a goal, not limit you by restricting what you can do. Study the chart, think about your goals, and follow your sense of what is right for you in arranging each room.

FIREPLACES

FIREPLACES ARE AUSPICIOUS AND CREATE WARMTH AND GOOD FEELING. They can, however, allow chi to escape right up the chimney and out of the house. Hanging a mirror over the fireplace will reflect the chi and send it back into the room, rather than letting it get away up the flue.

A frequently used fireplace may radiate too much energy. Flanking it with leafy plants will correct the abundance of heat, while creating an aesthetically pleasing effect in the room. This simple arrangement is based on the destructive cycle of the five elements, in which the earth, represented by the plant, stabilizes fire, the heat of the fireplace. But be sure not to place a small tree or woody plant next to the fireplace because the wood element feeds fire; you would wind up feeding the fire with wood, creating too much heat and energy in the room.

Avoid orienting all the furniture in the room toward the fireplace, because friendly interaction requires that at least some guests sit facing one another. Nor should any chair be put so close to the fireplace that the heat can be felt too strongly by anyone seated there. This is for obvious reasons of comfort, but also because the overheated person will be more likely to flare up in anger at the group.

ANTIQUE FURNITURE SHOULD BE CHOSEN WITH CAUTION BECAUSE IT may come with bad chi from previous owners. The best way to assess an antique before you buy it, according to Master Govert, is to place your hand on it and be quiet for a moment. If you are able to put yourself in a neutral state and not be caught up thinking how great this old table will look under the front window, you will experience some sort of reaction. You may have nothing more than a vague sensation, you may have a complete vision, or you may get good or bad vibes from the item. Whatever you feel, pay attention and don't take home anything that has given you a negative feeling. It's not necessary to avoid furniture that looks a little banged up and may be in need of restoring, as long as it passes the "vibes" test. Antique jewelry should also be chosen with care. Jewelry is an intensely personal item and carries the chi, good or bad, of previous owners. Before you purchase that lovely locket, ring, or antique brooch, give it the vibes test.

ART AND ANTIQUES

Modern art is at the other end of the decorating spectrum, but you should evaluate it in a similar fashion: How does a piece of art make you feel? You may want to put something vivid and bold in the living room because it makes you feel alert and lively. But you would not want to have anything with those qualities in the bedroom, where abstracts with a dreamlike quality would be most appropriate. Many feng shui experts advise against buying art strictly for investment purposes or just to collect the paintings of a certain artist. Master Govert advises his clients this way: "Buy art only if it somehow expresses what you aspire to. Carefully monitor the art you have in your place so that it moves in the direction you want to move."

Choose art that represents life and happiness. Art that depicts death or otherwise has negative energy should be avoided. Many people enjoy collecting and displaying masks, which can be dramatic and interesting as well as highly colorful. But don't display any mask unless you are knowledgeable about its origins or purposes. Mounting funeral masks on the wall of your wealth, career, or health area will yield negative consequences in any of these aspects of your life.

Make liberal use of the colors that say something about who you are or reflect your aspirations and your sensibility. If you are a teacher or aspire to academic success, decorate in blue greens, the color of the northeast, which governs knowledge and scholarly success. You may want to accent whatever color you use as your main shade with other colors that pick up on additional hopes, concerns, or family goals—black for business or career success, green for health and family life, or purple for wealth and fortune.

LIGHTING

A WELL-LIT ROOM IS GENERALLY A ROOM WITH GOOD CHI. BUT BE SURE to use lighting in an attractive way.

- Harsh overhead lights can be oppressive to the occupants and very unwelcoming to guests.
- Table lamps that create cozy pools of light will relax the room's inhabitants and create good feelings.
- Floor lamps can be used in any number of ways. They are practical for illuminating a dark section of the room and can be feng shui "fixes," shining upward to lift a sunken room or stimulating chi flow in a wealth corner.

Because it is such a public space, the living room is a yang room. The yang quality is embodied by the activity and brightness, which are ideal for a family and entertaining center. However, occasional touches of yin, which bring some softness (throw pillows), coolness (plants and light-blocking draperies), and attractive contrasts of dark colors with paler shades will help achieve the balance and harmony you are striving for.

THE DINING ROOM

THE CHINESE TAKE FOOD AND THE ART OF DINING VERY SERIOUSLY. Eating, they believe, feeds the spirit as well as the body. For this reason, the dining room should be arranged with the idea of enhancing the well-being of the diners, as well as promoting harmony and good feeling among them.

Nothing in the dining room should detract from a pleasant dining and conversational experience. The room should not be crammed with too much furniture, making those present feel they are in the way. If possible, the room should contain only the dining table, chairs, and a sideboard, so as to keep the focus on the food and conversation. The chairs and table should be very comfortable, permitting diners to linger for hours over the food and company. Paintings and scenic murals are appropriate for the dining room, but you should avoid loud or aggressive artwork, which calls attention to itself and removes the focus from the food and the people enjoying it. Following these simple rules will bring harmony to your family and dinner guests. Meals will be more pleasant and will contribute to overall happiness because good feng shui aids good digestion, which encourages the good health needed to achieve prosperity and a happy family life.

The location of the dining room and the kitchen are significant. It is said that if either room is too near the front door, guests will eat and run. If the dining room is too near the front door, the family will be greedy and preoccupied with eating! Children who live in these homes are said to think of food the moment they walk in the house and neglect their studies because they eat so much.

The most auspicious location for the dining room is east of the kitchen, because this compass point governs growth and health, the very aspects of living that food is intended to promote. But if your home doesn't happen to offer such a layout, don't worry; you can achieve good feng shui in your dining room through any of the various means presented here.

As in the living room, family members should sit with the backs of their chairs to the wall of the dining room, rather than to doors or windows. This arrangement ensures that they will be seated in the commanding position in their own homes. And in this place they will feel secure enough to be gracious and hospitable to their guests.

It is best if there are two entrances to the dining room so that chi can flow easily in and out again. If you have a dining room with only one door, don't crowd the table or chairs too close to it, and be sure to keep the entry free of other obstructions. If you have only a dining area, not a separate room, use a large plant or folding screen to create a second entrance, which will encourage the chi to flow smoothly in and out while it blocks distractions and unwanted views of the kitchen or living room. In any case, always strive to create an intimate atmosphere, one that encourages conversation and lingering at the table.

Obviously, the dining table and chairs are the most important furniture in the room. The most auspicious shapes for a table are round or octagonal. The round table is desirable because it is complete and has no "missing parts" or right angles. Octagonal tables are excellent because they suggest the ba-gua, the chart from the I Ching that is the foundation of feng shui. The self-containment of both shapes reflects heavenly blessings on all who sit at these tables.

Since south is acknowledged to be the most auspicious direction, you can show proper respect and courtesy to honored guests or the eldest family members by seating them so that they face south at a round table.

Square and rectangular tables are fine, too, as long as guests are never seated at the corners, where they can develop digestive problems as a result of the corner pointing straight at their middles as they eat. Guests are also likely to become cantankerous if seated against a corner because sha, or bad chi, will be racing along the corner's two right angles, stirring up ill feeling within the person seated in its path.

Dining chairs should always be set out in even numbers because luck comes in even numbers and single numbers represent loneliness. If you live alone, or if your family has an uneven number of people in it, add an extra chair. This will even out the numbers at the same time that it opens up the possibility of welcoming a friend or guest to your table at a moment's notice.

The dining room is one room in which to take full advantage of mirrors. They are excellent for reflecting the blessings of the family and creating an abundance of food and friends. Place mirrors so that they reflect the table and the guests seated at it. This way, you will double the number of your friends as well as your family's prosperity, represented by the food on the table.

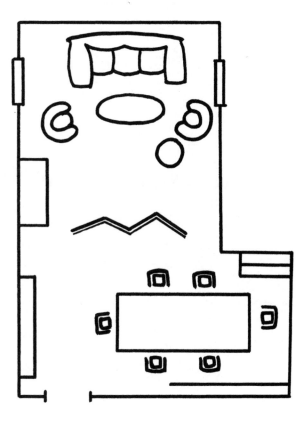

A folding screen not only enhances chi flow in an enclosed dining area, but also separates an L-shaped room into two rectangles, preventing dangling space.

S I X

THE KITCHEN
AND BATHROOM

THE MANDARIN CHINESE WORD FOR FOOD, TS'AI, SOUNDS LIKE THE word for "wealth." That tells you something right away about the importance of the kitchen in Chinese culture. (The Chinese, you may have already noticed, put great faith in homonyms.) A generously stocked refrigerator and pantry symbolize the family's wealth, and because the kitchen is the source of nourishment, a bountiful food supply also symbolizes the health, happiness, and general well-being of the family.

The feng shui practitioner Kathryn Metz is convinced that good feng shui in the kitchen enables the cook to prepare meals that supply strength and love in addition to basic sustenance. "When food is made with love, you carry this love with you throughout the day. It affects everything you do," she says.

It's no accident that people wind up gathering in the kitchen at parties—it's not just for the food. The real magnet for family and guests is the feeling of being nurtured as well as fed.

THE STOVE

THE PROPER PLACEMENT OF THE STOVE—OR, IN CHINESE HOMES, THE rice cooker—is critical to the feng shui of your entire home.

The stove should be positioned so that you don't have your back directly to the door while cooking, so you won't be surprised by anyone coming into the kitchen. If the person cooking is startled or rattled while at the stove, his or her mood will be affected, food preparation will be thrown off, and the family will suffer as a result.

If your stove is situated so that you do have your back to the door while cooking, install a mirror over the burners. Not only will this keep you from being taken by surprise, it can also bring fortune and good luck in business. The burners, with their instant access to fire and their vital function in the preparation of the household's food, symbolize the family's success at trade and business. A mirror over the stove doubles their number and increases the family's earnings. In addition, the mirror enlarges the kitchen and opens it up to the flow of good chi.

The stove must always be kept clean, with the burners working smoothly. Clogged burners will block the family's income potential, while greasy stovetops create problems for the family's health through neglect of proper hygiene. Using all the burners regularly, instead of habitually using the same one or two, will maximize the family's income. The heat and energy constantly passing through all these openings will keep the family's business prospects from growing cold.

The balance of yin and yang is more important in the kitchen than in any other room. In the kitchen you have two clashing elements, both of which are basic to the room's function: fire, which is yang, and water, which is yin. The stove should not be next to your sink because this mixes two conflicting elements on the same wall. If this is the arrangement in your kitchen, you can correct the problem without moving the stove by placing something metal or wood as a buffer between them. Common kitchen accessories such as a wooden cutting board or set of metal canisters would work well for this purpose.

In many Chinese homes a paper effigy of the kitchen god keeps watch on the family's behavior all year long. At Chinese New Year, families spread honey or other sweets on his mouth and set him on fire. This ensures that when the kitchen god arrives at the gates of heaven to make his annual report, he will say only sweet things about everyone in the household.

IN A KITCHEN (OR IN ANY ROOM), THE WALL WITH THE WINDOW THAT lets in the most light is the "facing" wall. Since metal is associated with the west and fire with the south, a perfect kitchen would face west (an auspicious direction for the metal appliances) with the stove on the south wall. You will want to be careful, however, not to combine too many elements associated with the south—such as the color red or images of birds—in your kitchen. And be wary of a south-facing kitchen because it can focus the fire element too intensely.

GENERAL
KITCHEN TIPS

One Los Angeles woman with a south-facing kitchen had developed the dangerous habit of forgetting to unplug the coffee pot when she left the house in the morning. She burned up several pots—and one almost took the entire kitchen with it. When the time came to redecorate her home, this woman was fortunate enough to hire a decorator who had considerable background in feng shui.

The decorator understood at once that an abundance of the fire element in the kitchen had caused the woman's frequent brushes with kitchen fires. He couldn't move the kitchen to a more auspicious part of the house, but he did have the woman install chrome toe kicks on the baseboards and remove a set of red dishes from the south-facing kitchen. The addition of metal counterbalanced the strong fire element, and removing the red dishes also took much of the excess heat from the room. In her newly decorated kitchen, the woman's dangerous forgetfulness vanished: the room's poor feng shui was no longer compounding the problem.

Kitchens facing north are less auspicious than those with other orientations, an idea that probably dates back to ancient China, where ill winds regularly blew noxious yellow dust down from Mongolia in the north. If your kitchen faces this direction, suspend wind chimes or a mobile near a window to keep the good chi swirling in a lively and healthful way through your kitchen.

No matter which way your kitchen faces, it should always be clean and airy. The best way to achieve this is to paint the room white. In Chinese culture, and in the practice of feng shui, white is a color with two very different connotations. Though it is the color of funerals and mourning, white is also a symbol of purity. Furthermore, white is appropriate because it is associated with the element metal and therefore is in harmony with the stove, refrigerator, and other appliances that are common in most kitchens.

As always, the flow of good chi is fundamental in the kitchen. An airy, well-lit kitchen will admit quantities of good chi. This good chi will find its way into the food you cook and improve the health, happiness, and good fortune of you and your family.

THE BATHROOM

THE BATHROOM PRESENTS A RATHER DELICATE SITUATION BECAUSE water, the fundamental element in this room, plays a dual role. It is essential for washing away dirt and eliminating impurities, but at the same time, water is *the* symbol of money. Because daily bathroom routines require flushing quantities of water out of the house, you must arrange this room carefully or your families finances could literally go down the drain!

The bathroom . . .

- should not face the front door, or else the occupants' wealth, along with the good chi that enters through the door, will be flushed away.
- should not be directly above the front entrance, because this arrangement portends disaster for the family.
- should not be in a central part of the house—that is, it should have at least one outside wall. This is partly a function of good ventilation. But this rule also stems from the belief that the center of the home should be the hub of activity, and thus is ideally the location of a living room or family room.

• should not be close to or above the kitchen. A bathroom above the kitchen means that waste is flushed past a key area of the home.

If your bathroom is located in the central part of the house or is close to the kitchen, hang a mirror outside the bathroom door to deflect the negative energy generated by either one of these placements.

If the bathroom faces the front door or is above the home's main entrance, put a small mirror at the base of the toilet. The mirror will gather and deflect the chi so that it, and the family's wealth, isn't flushed straight down and out the front door.

Ideally, the bathroom should be large enough to be functional, but not too spacious. It should be painted a pale color and kept free of clutter to encourage chi to move quickly through the room.

The toilet should not be easily visible from the bathroom door. Locating the toilet behind the door is good, as is putting it in an alcove. If yours is immediately visible from the door, put up a curtain or cabinet or add a floor plant to shield the toilet from view.

Although many feng shui masters consider the bathroom to be the least auspicious room in the home and frown on overly elaborate arrangements, there is no reason it should not be a pleasant room. "A bathroom is a retreat," says the interior designer Joan Malter Osburn. "You should feel relaxed and comfortable while you're in there." So while you are paying attention to chi flow and the rules of feng shui for the bathroom, feel free to make the room as pleasant as possible.

Use soft, pastel-colored towels to bring the proper color elements into play. Green is a restful color that aids the digestive process while it promotes health. Blue is associated with the oceans, lakes, and rivers; it will help keep the water moving briskly and discourage plumbing problems, while it encourages good cash flow.

The sink, tub, toilet, and drains make the bathroom the most yin room in the house. Some of the characteristics of yin, you may remember, are dampness and darkness. Because of this room's strong yin quality, adding elements of yang will balance the room and improve its feng shui. To do this, add touches of bright color to the bathroom, or put some candles around. Lighted candles will supply the balance of yang by adding the element of fire while giving aesthetically pleasing illumination.

Keep drains covered as much as possible and keep the toilet closed when it's not in use. If the water is flushed away when the toilet is open, your luck and money will drain away with it, right out of the house.

YOUR STUDY AND OFFICE

JUST AS THE FENG SHUI OF YOUR HOME CAN AFFECT YOUR HEALTH, happiness, and prosperity, proper feng shui in your study or office will affect your concentration, creativity, and mental abilities. This is why your office arrangement and desk orientation directly affect your academic, business, or commercial achievements.

Whether your home office is used to run a business, to pay household bills, or to read and study, you'll want to be able to think clearly and focus your concentration while in this room. The feng shui of your office, including the placement of your desk, will strongly influence all outcomes: you may prosper or flounder, you may command respect or be taken advantage of, you may make good decisions or bad.

No matter where your office is, at home or at a work site, doing your best is always critical in a work environment because the results of your efforts are constantly being measured, by you, your boss and coworkers, or your clients or customers. This is one reason why the application of feng shui principles are often at their most rewarding in an office setting.

Sharon, a Southern California screenwriter, developed writer's block when she redecorated her home and moved her office to another room in her house. Her first office had been converted from a spare bedroom and she had worked well there, but over the years the room became a storage space for furniture, exercise equipment, and other odds and ends, and began to feel crowded. After creating an elaborate new work space in a different room of the house, she ran into trouble. "I realized that I wasn't spending any time in the room and I was struggling with writing," she said. "I procrastinated—it just didn't feel right."

She was puzzled and asked a friend who was an interior designer what might be done to improve the room. The designer suggested that Sharon call a feng shui practitioner, who told Sharon that the new office was cut off from the flow of energy, or chi, because of its location in a dangling wing of the house. Since her home was large enough, the solution to the room's poor feng shui was to abandon the new office and move back to the original spot. The "new" office was turned into a library and reading room, where less energy, and therefore less chi, was required.

Next, the decorator and the feng shui practitioner worked together to rearrange the old office in a way that was more conducive to Sharon's creative work. One of the first tasks was to clear out clutter. This encouraged circulation of chi and allowed Sharon to focus on projects and think clearly without distraction. The next job was to put her large, curving desk in the southeast corner of the room, allowing Sharon at various times to face east (which governs growth, youth, and prosperity), southeast (for wealth and creativity), and south (for fame, fortune, and sincerity) from her desk chair. All of these qualities are now being channeled into Sharon's writing.

THE LOCATION OF YOUR DESK IS THE SINGLE MOST IMPORTANT FENG shui consideration in the workplace. At home, your desk follows only your bed and stove in the importance of its placement.

DESK PLACEMENT

Generally speaking, your desk should be in a "commanding" position: you should always face the door and you should sit far enough inside the office to see the whole room from your desk. If you sit with your back to the door, you will not be sufficiently alert to your surroundings and may be surprised by people entering your office as well as by the things they have to say. Kristin Frederickson, the art director at a small New York publishing house, says she thinks it's almost impossible for anyone to work well with his or her back to the door. "There's such a powerful energy about not knowing what's going on behind your back," she says. "If you work that way, you are going to have paranoid energy around you, and your paranoia will be felt by coworkers."

If you sit too close to the entrance door, you won't have control of the room; those sitting farther inside the office will have a better grasp of the business. Facing the office door from a seat well into the

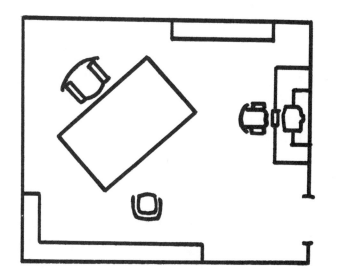

The "command" position for desk placement

room, you will have mastery over all you observe. You will think more clearly, your judgment will be sound, and as a result your authority will be respected.

If it isn't possible to arrange your desk so that you face the door, remedy this by hanging a small mirror over your desk so that you can see the door reflected in it. If you face the door but are unable to see the rest of the room, use a mirror to improve your view.

TIPS FOR YOUR BUSINESS OFFICE

- The location of the manager's or boss's office is the most important factor in determining the overall success of any business enterprise. The most favorable site for this important office is farthest from the front door. Away from the hustle and bustle, the manager will see the big picture and not be distracted by the minutia of daily transactions. This distance also allows the manager time to contemplate decisions that might be made hastily if he or she were too closely involved with the press of activity coming in from the street. With the perspective and serenity that this office position provides, the manager will have maximum control over the operation of the business as well as good concentration and decision-making ability. His or her authority will be respected.

- The boss's desk should not be close to the office door or he or she will not have sufficient control over the operation and will not be treated with proper deference. Similarly, workers whose desks are farther inside the office than the boss's are likely to be insubordinate; they will feel more in command than their superior.

- The best spot for the manager's desk within his or her office is kitty-corner to the office door. This position provides maximum control and is also most auspicious for bringing financial success to the business because chi will have ample space to circulate around the manager's desk, bringing fortune and good luck.

Do you wish your telephone would ring more often? Do you wait for calls that don't come? Try hanging a crystal ball over the phone and see if the telephone traffic in your household doesn't pick up considerably once the chi starts to spin around the hanging crystal.

If you have just the opposite problem—too many calls— setting a heavy stone next to the telephone will stabilize the area and reduce the energy flowing into the instrument. This will keep it from ringing so often.

- For a more powerful presence at meetings, try to take the chair facing the door. This posture will make you highly sensitive to the dynamics of the room. Don't sit with your back to a window. A solid wall behind you will provide more backing for your ideas and lend authority to your presence.
- Move desks so that you don't directly face your office mates while seated at your desks. A face-to-face seating arrangement can cause confrontations between coworkers.
- Jutting corners in the workplace, especially if they point toward your back, will contribute to disruptive office politics. A young paralegal at a large law firm felt he was the victim of backstabbing and had trouble getting along with superiors and colleagues until he noticed that an angled wall pointed at his back. He set a floor plant in front of it and his relationships with coworkers improved.
- Plants and flowers also contribute to the good feng shui of any office or study. You will enjoy a more harmonious working environment and receive the benefits of healthy, smooth-flowing chi if you leaven the atmosphere with living things and occasional enhancements such as a bowl of goldfish—remember, they symbolize money—or pleasant-sounding wind chimes.

OFFICE LOCATION

THE BEST LOCATION FOR YOUR STUDY OR HOME OFFICE DEPENDS ON how you plan to use the room. If you are running a business or otherwise earning your living from your home, an office facing south, the direction that governs fame, fortune, and sincerity, will help ensure your good reputation and success. If the room is a study for you or a school-aged child, the best results will come from a northeastern orientation because that direction controls knowledge and scholarly success.

If you aren't able to set up the study in a room with the orientation you would prefer, you still have some good options. If possible, place the desk itself in the southern or northeastern corner of the room. Enhance the area with an appropriate color—red for the south and blue green for the northeast. For the southern location, you may also want to add a representation of the element fire. You can do this with candles, especially red ones, or even a picture of a red phoenix, the legendary bird that rises from its own ashes. In any case, remember to arrange the desk so that your back is not to the doorway.

OFFICE EQUIPMENT

COMPUTERS, TELEPHONES, FAX MACHINES, AND FILING CABINETS should all be placed in their most auspicious areas. Metal equipment will generally do well on a west wall, because this direction has metal as its element. However, you can choose from various placement options to suit your own particular requirements. For example, the interior designer Annie Kelly chose a southeast corner for her office equipment: "The easiest thing to do is to put office equipment in a corner anyway, so you might as well put it in the wealth corner!" She put her fax machine there, along with a light and a plant "for good measure." Has it helped? "So far," she says, "so good." Bear in mind that there will often be a variety of choices for the best placement of an item. Focus on your primary goal—whether wealth, reputation, or knowledge—and arrange the room accordingly.

LIGHTING

GOOD LIGHT IS IMPORTANT FOR AN OFFICE, BOTH FOR ILLUMINATING your work and for creating good feng shui. Bright lights help promote healthy, flowing chi. Glare, on the other hand, is a distraction and a source of bad chi, or sha. Be especially careful that glare doesn't hit your face. Ideally, windows should be to the side of your desk. If it is unavoidable for you to sit so that glare comes into your line of vision, hang a multifaceted crystal at the window to disperse the sha from this glare and create good chi.

BOOKSHELVES ARE A NATURAL AND CONVENIENT ADDITION TO ANY study or office. But you must be careful to arrange them so that the edges of the shelves don't create cutting blades or poison arrows directed toward you while you work. The flat planes that come together to form a corner conduct energy very quickly, turning it into sha, which forms menacing arrows. Prevent this dangerous situation by using enclosed bookcases instead of open shelving. Doors enclosing cabinets and shelves will block off the edges and prevent harmful energy from slicing at you while helping reduce the clutter and distractions in your office.

STORAGE

CLEAR THINKING WILL BE OBSCURED AND CREATIVITY WILL BE BLOCKED if books, papers, and bills are stacked all around your desk. According to the feng shui practitioner Louis Audet, all extraneous items in your office are sending messages and speaking to you: "Look at me! Read this! Pay this!" Keeping your office free of clutter is vital to your creativity as well as to your ability to concentrate. Eliminating distractions will increase your overall success.

Steve, a California elementary-school teacher, improved his financial situation by fixing up his home office according to feng shui principles. His office was a mess, and "that described my finances." He uncluttered and rearranged the room, paying special attention to the "wealth" corner, which he enhanced with an aquarium. So far the results have been modest but positive. "I'm not wealthier," he said, "but I'm more organized and I have more control over my finances."

The relationship between feng shui and finance can be seen on a much grander scale in buildings belonging to any number of large, multinational corporations. The headquarters of the Hongkong and Shanghai Banking Corporation in Hong Kong is a famous example of the application of feng shui principles on a grand scale. Reputed to be one of the most technologically advanced skyscrapers in the world, the forty-seven-story building was sited and constructed according to

CLUTTER AND CLARITY

A fish tank can be a magnet for wealth and prosperity. The fish themselves symbolize never-ending abundance (there are always more fish in the sea!)—in fact, li, the Chinese word for "carp," sounds the same as the word for "prosperity."

the strictest feng shui principles. Many visitors wonder at the odd angle of escalators that lead from the plaza level to the main banking floor. The moving stairs appear to have been placed at random, but in fact they are situated exactly to conduct chi and wealth evenly throughout the structure. Moreover, it is no accident that the building faces the sea and has Victoria Peak at its back, a position that confers on this financial giant the benefits of these highly auspicious land forms. The mountain provides support and protection for the corporation's business ventures, while the ocean invites wealth to flow into the building.

In your home office you may not enjoy the luxury of a nearby ocean like the one near the Hongkong and Shanghai Bank, but a fountain somewhere near the front of your home will achieve the same effect. On the advice of one of its Asian-American managers, a Motorola office in Phoenix, Arizona, installed not one but two waterfalls at its entrance and now boasts of a brisk business climate.

From Hong Kong to Phoenix, serious-minded businesspeople have learned that using feng shui to achieve harmony and balance in the office pays major dividends. It doesn't matter whether you work alone at home or in a large, multinational corporation; you will find that your professional life, and the prosperity and vitality of your overall business, will reap the benefits of your practice of feng shui.

EIGHT

THE GARDEN

ACHIEVING BALANCE AND HARMONY IS THE GOAL OF A CHINESE GAR-den, whether you're working with a large backyard, a small patio, or even just a window box. Your garden must be planted with the same attention you pay to the inside of the building if it is to contribute to the balance and harmony of your home.

Observing the rules of feng shui in designing your garden will enable you to balance the yin and yang of your property. This is because buildings, with their wood, concrete, steel, bricks, and other solid construction materials, are yang, while earth, plants, flowers, and ponds are yin. The elements of yin and yang are interdependent, each requiring the other to achieve the goal of the Tao, or "the way": balance between these two great universal forces.

The Pulitzer Prize–winning American playwright and Nobel laureate Eugene O'Neill had a deep interest in Eastern thought. O'Neill built his Northern California home in the hills above the tiny town of Danville and called it Tao House in honor of the Chinese philosophy of self-cultivation through following "the way" or "the path." This frequently visited site incorporates elements of feng shui in an eclectic blend of Eastern and Western design elements.

The garden in particular is a wonderful example of a Western courtyard that incorporates in its design principles of Eastern philosophy. The courtyard includes typical Chinese elements such as a rock garden, where O'Neill meditated, and gently curving paths that meander through the grounds like streams. The paths are narrow to encourage solitude and quiet meditation and to discourage people from strolling two abreast, chatting. Also, in a style more Eastern than Western, the garden is planted predominantly with white blossoms: azaleas, star jasmine, geraniums, and oleanders provide simple accents for the greenery. In the spring, the scene is dominated by a wisteria vine with delicate white blooms that droop from the verandas of the Spanish-style house.

O'Neill himself lovingly tended a centuries-old oak tree that grows just outside the main gate. In fact, garden chores like trimming bushes and tacking vines to walls were among O'Neill's favorite pastimes. This may have been because the tasks allowed some fresh air and physical activity into the reclusive playwright's otherwise sedentary existence. The grounds of Tao House helped create balance in O'Neill's life.

DESIGNING A CHINESE GARDEN

A WELL-DESIGNED GARDEN IN THE CHINESE STYLE DIFFERS IN SOME important ways from Western notions of what makes a beautiful garden. If you would like to create a Chinese garden, here are a few guidelines to keep in mind.

- Western gardeners may strive to impress with the color and variety of flowers, but Chinese gardeners instead go for subtlety and balance. Masses of flowers creating a blaze of color

Guardian trees

are not considered good feng shui. Delicately hued flowers or various colors of green are prized instead.

- Most Chinese gardens include rocks, either arranged in groups or standing alone. They are included for the beauty of their forms and their textures. The hard rock contrasts with the smoothness and softness of the plants and earth, contributing to the yin/yang balance of the landscape.

- Large trees are usually planted as a backdrop to the overall garden design. Three or more trees planted in a row will serve as guardians for the building and grounds. If you live in an area where the land is flat, trees in this arrangement make a good substitute for the protection that hills or mountains might otherwise offer. Guardian trees should be evergreens so that their year-round fullness will provide uninterrupted protection. They should be healthy and vigorous growers, since spindly or diseased trees are not good guardians and can attract negative energy with their sickly nature.

- Fountains with flowing water create an abundance of good feng shui. The movement of the water attracts chi, while the flow of the water symbolizes cash flow and does much to encourage prosperity.

- Pools and ponds are also excellent for feng shui, especially if

they contain large healthy fish, or even a tortoise. Gold or silver fish, representing gold and silver coins, are important prosperity symbols, while the slow and steady tortoise is the
epitome of longevity and a strong portent of long life for those
who keep him.

- If you have a pool or pond, it should curve toward your building so that the water appears to embrace it. In this position the
water will protect the building. If it curves away, the water will
form an unlucky arrow shooting sha in your direction.

- Mix shapes and sizes of plants in your garden so that no one
tree or plant grouping overwhelms the others. This is an element of balance.

- Paths should curve gently through your garden, echoing the
natural movement of chi. But they should never be twisted or
spiral, as these shapes suggest snakes, unwelcome guests in any
garden.

- Less is more in a Chinese garden. A densely planted garden
plot will be less interesting to the eye than one with a few interesting plants laid out artfully.

- Above all, your garden should look as natural as possible.
Though it should be carefully planned, it should never
appear contrived, but should seem to have occurred in that
spot all on its own. Chinese gardeners prefer indigenous
rather than exotic flowers and plants to achieve this natural
look.

A well-tended garden serves a practical purpose. According to
the feng shui consultant Marsha Golangco, "Good landscaping is
like clothes for the house—very important to its overall appearance."
By attracting and helping to circulate good chi, a pleasant exterior to
your home will be an important element in the overall quality of your
home's feng shui.

FINAL THOUGHTS

THE CHINESE HAVE A SAYING ABOUT THE FORCES THAT PLAY A ROLE IN shaping our lives: "First comes destiny; second is luck; third, feng shui; fourth, philanthropy; and fifth, education."

You've begun to take control of these forces—and of the direction your life can take—through this introduction to feng shui. By reading this book you've educated yourself. By putting feng shui to work in your home, you'll be assisting your family in achieving its goals, whether financial, academic, or relationship-oriented. Using the principles of feng shui, you will make your home a welcome place for guests, and this first step toward philanthropy will pay off.

Whenever you get the feeling that things have taken a turn for the worse, focus on the problems confronting you. After careful thought about what you would like to change, apply the principles of feng shui: move a bed or plant; paint a particular room blue; hang a flute or wind chimes. Do whatever seems appropriate to your situation. Then you'll notice that feng shui is creating new solutions for you and moving your life in positive directions, along paths you may only have dreamed were possible.

FURTHER READING

Blofield, John, editor. *I Ching: The Book of Changes.* New York: Viking, 1991.

Eitel, Ernst. *Feng Shui, or the Rudiments of Natural Science in China.* Hong Kong, 1873.

Keswick, Maggie. *The Chinese Garden.* New York: St. Martin's Press, 1986.

Lip, Evelyn. *Feng Shui: A Layman's Guide to Chinese Geomancy.* Union City, Cal.: Heian International, 1986.

———. *Feng Shui for Business.* Union City, Cal.: Heian International, 1990.

———. *Feng Shui for the Home.* Union City, Cal.: Heian International, 1990.

Rossbach, Sarah. *Feng Shui: The Chinese Art of Placement.* New York: Penguin, 1983.

———. *Interior Design with Feng Shui.* New York: E. P. Dutton, 1987.

Rybczynski, Witold. *The Most Beautiful House in the World.* New York: Viking, 1990.

Too, Lillian. *Applied Feng Shui*. Malaysia: Konsept Lagenda SdN BhD, 1993.

————. *Feng Shui*. Malaysia: Konsept Lagenda SdN BhD, 1993.

————. *Practical Applications of Feng Shui*. Malaysia: Konsept Lagenda SdN BhD, 1994.

Walters, Derek. *The Feng Shui Handbook: A Practical Guide to Chinese Geomancy*. San Francisco: Thorson's, 1991.

————. *Feng Shui: Perfect Placing for Your Happiness and Prosperity*. London: Asiapac Books, 1988.

Waring, Phillipa. *The Way of Feng Shui*. London: Souvenir Press, 1993.

Wong, Angi Ma. *The Practical Feng Shui Chart*. Palos Verdes, Cal.: Pacific Heritage Books, 1992.

————. *Target: The U.S.–Asian Market*. Palos Verdes, Cal.: Pacific Heritage Books, 1993.

Kirsten Lagatree is an award-winning writer and radio producer. Her work has appeared frequently in the *Los Angeles Times* and other southern California publications. Lagatree has a master's degree in humanities from the University of Chicago, and she currently lives in northern Virginia with her husband and two cats.

Angi Ma Wong is an intercultural consultant and feng shui practitioner in the Los Angeles area. She is the developer of the first do-it-yourself feng shui kit, as well as the author of *Night of the Red Moon* and the award-winning *Target: The U.S.–Asian Market: A Practical Guide to Doing Business.*